JAZZ AS CRITIQUE

Fumi Okiji

ADORNO AND BLACK EXPRESSION REVISITED

STANFORD UNIVERSITY PRESS
STANFORD, CALIFORNIA

Stanford University Press
Stanford, California

Printed in the United States of America on acid-free, archival-quality paper

Library of Congress Cataloging-in-Publication Data
Names: Okiji, Fumi, 1976- author.
Title: Jazz as critique : Adorno and black expression revisited / Fumi Okiji.
Description: Stanford, California : Stanford University Press, 2018. | Includes bibliographical references and index.
Identifiers: LCCN 2017045420 | ISBN 9781503602021 (cloth : alk. paper) | ISBN 9781503605855 (pbk.) | ISBN 9781503605862 (epub)
Subjects: LCSH: Jazz—History and criticism. | Jazz—Philosophy and aesthetics. | African American musicians. | African American aesthetics. | Aesthetics, Black. | Adorno, Theodor W., 1903-1969—Aesthetics.
Classification: LCC ML3508 .O45 2018 | DDC 781.65/117—dc23
LC record available at https://lccn.loc.gov/2017045420

Typeset by Bruce Lundquist in 10/14 Minion Pro

When the founders of the Humanist Union invited me to become a member, I replied that "I might possibly be willing to join if your club had been called an inhuman union, but I could not join one that calls itself 'humanist.'"

–Theodor W. Adorno

CONTENTS

ACKNOWLEDGMENTS

The generous support of the Arts and Humanities Research Council (UK); of Royal Holloway, University of London; and of Northwestern University's Weinberg School of Arts and Sciences and School of Communications gave me the freedom to study for this book and to write it.

I'm immensely appreciative of the encouragement, comments, and thoughtful criticism of colleagues on both sides of the Atlantic—in particular, Andrew Bowie, Kwami T. Coleman, Ryan Dohoney, Jon Hughes, Jonathan Impett, Daniel Matlin, Anna Parkinson, Ben Piekut, Guthrie Ramsey, and Christopher Wells. Special thanks to Penny Deutscher, who helped name the book. I am truly indebted to Dhanveer Singh Brar, Ciarán Finlayson, Sam Fisher, and Lucie Mercier for going out of their way to read chapters from earlier versions, to which they responded with such care (toward me as much as the writing). I thank Fred Moten for his encouragement and support, Sabine Broeck for her counsel and friendship. I pay tribute to musicians on the London scene and, in particular, to my collaborators over the years: much love and admiration to Olie Brice, Ben Davis, Roy Dodds, Zac Gvi, Stuart Hall, Stefano Kalonaris, Idris Rahman, Orphy Robinson, Seb Rochford, Noel Taylor, Fred Thomas, Pat Thomas, Cleveland Watkiss, and Trevor Watkis. I am so very grateful to Lorenzo Simpson, Alex Weheliye, and an anonymous reviewer—the book is so much better for their attention and comment. I also thank Emily-Jane Cohen, Marthine Desiree Satris, Faith Wilson Stein, Joe Abbott, and others at Stanford University Press for their patience and for helping bring this book to fruition. Many thanks to Josh Rutner for his outstanding editing and index.

I am forever grateful to Tania Kausmally for being my partner-in-hope/despair during the writing of the first draft. The other folk up on the West Hill—Hannah Bîcat, Greig Burgoyne, Louise Burgess, Nuala McNurdle, Steve Painter, and Tina Zambetakis—I must thank for keeping me sane. I miss them, so much! My Evanston friends, Yulia Borisova, Yali Dekel, and Jody Koizumi, really looked after me during the seemingly endless closing stages of the project.

To my late mother, Aduke Akeju Okiji, and to my father, Akinboye Okiji; my sister, Sade Okiji Milton; and brothers, Femi Okiji and Gbenga Okiji: I have been searching, without success, for words to express my affection and appreciation. Thank you, fam.

To my loves, Zeno, Atti, and Ben: How lucky I am that you're here with me.

JAZZ AS CRITIQUE

INTRODUCTION

There is a short passage in the middle of Jaki Byard's solo on "Fables of Faubus" that begins with the pianist playing a stuttered quotation from "Yankee Doodle" (perhaps reminiscing about an early piano lesson). A descending bass line pulls listeners away from the practice room toward an insistent common blues trope. Byard moves on quickly—prematurely, it seems at the time—to the opening phrase of Frédéric Chopin's "Marche funèbre," completing the medley. The triptych in itself is rich with inference: the sandwiching of the blues between child's play and death; the play of time—from the out of time / lost time of nursery rhythm, through a slight pulsating push, to a laid-back swing, perverting the funereal march. There is much to think through. Yet it is its blues part that most caught my interest. As Byard continues in a style more in keeping with the recent modal developments in jazz harmony, that phrase plays on in the imagination. So it is immensely satisfying to hear Mingus resuscitate it verbatim. This unleashes a staggered shout chorus of response begun by Eric Dolphy's bass clarinet, chased an octave higher by Clifford Jordan on tenor saxophone. The phrase is accompanied by interpellations on muted trumpet by Johnny Coles and, soon after, by Mingus's vocals and then other band members' sniggers of assent, exclamation, huffs, squeals, and sighs. This supporting contribution soon becomes the focus, pulling Dolphy and Jordan into its vocal(like) interlocution. In the meantime, the rhythm section finally succeeds in luring Byard away from his modal reverie, morphing into a frisky rhythm-and-blues shuffle.

These thoughts begin with the Charles Mingus Sextet at Cornell University.[1] Listening to a recording of the concert the band gave in 1964, I was struck by how well their work—that is, their sociomusical play—resembled ideas of a progressive, empathetic mode of sociality suggested by critical theorist Theodor Adorno. While adhering to a strict negativism, which prohibits "utopia [being] positively pictured," Adorno's work on the critical potential of art offers something in the order of a code of conduct, a guide to how people might go about "arrang[ing] their thoughts and actions" to resist a world in which Auschwitz could occur—an essential precondition to any utopic future.[2] He rejects the idea that art can provide a blueprint of a future society, that it can be adapted for social or political purposes; in fact, even when driven by honorable intention, our propensity to extract utility, to quantify and, ultimately, to profit from that which is brought within our purview, compounds the totalizing tendencies such praxis claims to counter. Yet lying just beneath the surface of Adorno's writing on art is an unremitting address of the ethical disposition required to bring about such revolution.

Adorno submits the idea that music, when coupled with critical reflection, offers, for all intents and purposes, a social theory, constituted by two distinct but interlocking areas of exploration. First, according to Adorno, the contradictions, fissures, falsehoods, and other structuring conditions of modern and contemporary life can be read from a musical work, which is, after all, despite its relative autonomy, also social fact. Expressive work cannot help but partake of societal dysfunction, even when—and perhaps *especially* when—an artist is committed to countering these dehumanizing conditions through his or her work content. The second of these areas of study is concerned with the notion that a musical work, through the way it comes together in composition and unfolds in performance, points to a way for us to be together in the world, against the world's tendency to reduce us, qualitatively. On various levels of structuration a composition is formed through a productive tension between particularity and communion. The composer wrestles with an active pool of found musical material; chords, intervals, feel, and generic sensibility may all pull in divergent directions. The single note similarly stakes its claim to significance against the phrase or chord in which it falls. The various elements of the work tussle and wed—an unstable, never-to-be-taken-for-granted union—holding on to distinction as they come together in cooperation. Absolute synthesis, if such a virtue were obtainable in practice, would not produce artistic work. The unwieldiness of particulars—how they jump out, protrude, and threaten to unravel the forming or unfolding piece—is definitive of such work and artifacts. Indeed, as Adorno reveals, artistic work and the products of that labor "speak" to us "by virtue of the communication of everything *particular* in them." The embrace of these potential agitators, the preservation of "their diffuse, divergent and contradictory condition . . . is the unfolding of truth."[3] This respect for particularity within a work's musical material and event, even as the various aspects come together in a discrete space and transpire temporally, presents an attitude that has little place outside of the arts. It is a way of being that struggles in other spheres of living invariably driven and dependent on instrumentality and violent integration. These are the ideas Mingus's ensemble helped me recall.

The sextet is hooked up and conversant with a social world with which it has a burdensome relationship. As a group of black men, the musicians show up in it only insofar as they confirm, augment, or rejuvenate extramural presuppositions pertaining to "the black"—a category used to control people of African descent and a marker of the outer limit of what can be considered human, one of the restricted ways black folk show up in the general social field—or the extent to which their activity and what they produce can be made appropriate for, and be synthesized into, the mainstream. This degraded involvement is enforced, which is to say that both the degradation and how this mainstream imagining is used takes place with or without black consent. Although key texts chronicling the malevolent underbelly of modernity—such as Adorno's—fail to manage more than a cursory glance, and most often contribute to a broad denial of black humanity, a tradition of black radical thought has offered a compelling case about why the formation of the black subject, which is always to say the inauguration and continuance of its subordination, should be considered the nucleus of modernity. This collective critique shows the near-silence of European and Euro-American humanities to be part of a comprehensive program that works to eliminate, or at least obscure, blackness. The near-silence labors as hard as the overtly racist. *Jazz as Critique* is enabled by a chorus of thinkers—Saidiya Hartman, Hortense Spillers, Nahum Chandler, Fred Moten, Stefano Harney, Jared Sexton, Nathaniel Mackey, and Frank Wilderson, to name only the most significant—who have shown how it is that blackness is structurally incapable of world-making, how black subjectivity was encoded from the start with irresolvable contradictions, how this subject is caught between the denial of American/human home and the active dissolution of African origin, and how black expression is never innocuous but rather both complicit in its own subjugation and a critical weapon deployed against it.

Black life's incapacity to extend meaningfully through the objects and people of its environment is pronounced on each stratum of modern and contemporary society. The election of African Americans to the highest of public offices provides a depressing relief of appropriate black incursion, against which this inability is cast. Similarly, activist Marissa Johnson's challenge to potential allies of Black Lives Matter to not just appreciate appropriated products of the expression but to "love black people" is an astute rejoinder to those who present alleged black cultural dominance as evidence of forthcoming equality.[4] Even if I were to accept that a compensatory social currency is facilitated by ubiquitous (appropriated) black cultural forms (which I do not), there would still remain an overwhelming need for society at large to know and share (in) the *life* of black people. In CCTV footage a black boy, racing through an urban landscape, most often becomes visible by way of his potential criminality (increasingly this is "countered" by mobile-phone video in which he shows up—with similar inaccuracy—as "the victim"). It takes a keen eye to draw to the fore from those grainy frames "a boy at play in himself, and perhaps with the image of himself."[5] To see and recognize everyday black living requires X-ray vision. Blackness may well be a thing not yet known, as Fred Moten tells us, and it is unclear how the world could ever know it without internal collapse. But black life *is* lived, and particularly where it comes up against its appropriated and sanctioned mainstream images and uses, where it misshapes the categorical smoothness of race, it provides invaluable insight. In its contradictory subjecthood—human enough for governance but too black for admittance to the "household of humanity"—such life rhymes with what Adorno understands to be the double character of radical art, rejecting what it is unable to rid itself of through critical immersion.[6] It could well be argued that black life is necessarily an artistic undertaking, although questions pertaining to that do not drive this present study. What *is* suggested here, however, is that black expressive work cannot but help shed light on black life's (im)possibilities.[7]

Black music is sociomusical play. It is not so much that it represents black life or an alternative human future; rather, it demonstrates to us how to acquit ourselves toward blackness (and toward another world). It shows us how we might go about dispositioning ourselves, so that we might know how it feels to be a conflicted subject—both human and inhuman, American and black (African), and both "the black" and heterogeneous, fecund blackness. Holding contradictory positions, and the playful negotiations of these, is what is revealed in the recapitulation of Jaki Byard's blues riff described at the start of this chapter.

Byard's fellow players gravitate toward that node of significance. Their contributions thicken and deform it—initially by merely repeating the riff verbatim and then through more deliberate deconstruction. The performance allows us to glimpse a way to listen to, to be with, and to speak as part of a gathering of deviates. It demonstrates how unfettered, poorly regulated black life congregates in distinction. We are able to sneak a listen beyond the racial clod that organizes black excursions into mainstream spaces, of which discourse on jazz performance, such as we have here, must be included. The musicians are "at play in themselves," but they are also at play with the image or concept the world has of them. Their interlocution reflects, and is perhaps even facilitated by, the constant negotiations between their everyday life and that of the "hung, drawn-and-quartered" extramural portrayal. And at the risk of a charge of infinite regress, it could be argued that this burden is the foundational condition of blackness. The riff recalled by Byard (and again by Mingus) is a node of significance to which contribution gathers; and, in a slight shift of emphasis, it is also a token or symbol of an inescapable collectivity in displacement, an "abeyance of [the] closure" between appearance in the general social field and the life that imagining routinely suppresses.[8] The riff can be understood as a sacrificial amulet, an ever-forming, ever-vandalized effigy of "the black." While on, a distinct but imbricating register, the flashes of eschatological utopia that we hear in the sociomusical play take us, momentarily, into a blackened atmosphere "beyond space, time, causality, and individuation." According to Adorno, it is "in [these] emotional shocks of aesthetic experience" that the human "self peeps out for a moment over the walls of the prison that it itself is."[9]

The explorations in this study rest on the idea that black life cannot help but be lived as critical reflection. One need not be politically committed to question the integrity of the world. Blackness is a mode of existence in which the disjuncture between the reality of one's everyday living and the ways one is understood by society at large is so pronounced that the former must be considered an impossibility or a lie in order to preserve the latter. Enabled by, but in animated debate with, Adorno's thoughts on the notion of a social theory being offered by Western art, I propose that jazz is also capable of reflecting critically on the contradictions from which it arises—indeed, that it is compelled to do so.[10] Art embraces what the world cannot or will not accommodate, Adorno tells us. It gives voice to that which has been silenced or excluded, either willfully or through negligence. In a rejoinder to Adorno's European selectivity I will show how jazz, too, rejects "categorical determinations stamped on the empirical."[11] This book explores the idea that jazz—the music Adorno considered archetypically affirmative of the failed Enlightenment project and insufficiently autonomous to mount effective critique of it—is capable of contributing to a "model of a possible praxis" that shows a gathering constituted by the play, the wrestling and cooperation, of disparate parts. I am less interested in speculating on a utopian alternative than in explicating how jazz gives us access to a conflicted subject that will not cohere but rather is in a state of constant rejuvenation through the unstable, generative relations of its disparate ways.[12]

Why Adorno?

Krin Gabbard assures us that "while Miriam Hansen has brilliantly constructed a positive aesthetics of cinema out of Adorno's largely negative writings on film, no one is likely to tease a corresponding jazz aesthetic out of essays such as 'Perennial Fashion—Jazz.'"[13] Jazz studies' engagement with Adorno has been largely confined to the debate over his provocative linking of the music to the machinery of capitalistic cultural production. In dedicated texts such as "On Jazz," published in German in 1936, and "Perennial Fashion," which first appeared some seventeen years later, as well as in his treatment of the form within essays such as "On the Social Situation of Music" and "On the Fetish-Character of Music and the Regression of Listening," Adorno details his objections to what he views as an embodiment of the "administered life" of late capitalism, a synecdoche that speaks on behalf of the entire culture industry.[14] The publication of an English translation of "On Jazz" in 1989, which happened to coincide with the "contextual turn" within jazz studies, has resulted in a burgeoning of interest in Adorno's critique. Among the most astute of recent responses is Robert Witkin's, which, alongside an insightful rehearsal of the debate, reaches beyond well-established battle lines to suggest that, far from dismissing jazz as an inconsequential irritant, Adorno's attentiveness was due, in part, to the music's questioning the exceptionalism of Austro-German and critical formalism. Witkin writes: "The very claim that jazz music was good music, that it was serious and creative as well as being informal and primitive, posed a formidable challenge to the sociological and musicological theses that Adorno was advancing in respect of twentieth-century modernist music. Adorno's implacable opposition to jazz has to be seen in the context of these claims."[15] This is stunning speculation but, in light of the discussions of this book, also compelling. Furthermore, the all but unachievable preconditions required to instigate a genuine revolution bring Adorno's underdefined utopian ideal (which we might say would reside in these preconditions, as much as in any "No-Such-Place" beyond) very close to Jared Sexton's striking assertion that "the most radical negation of the anti-black world is the most radical affirmation of a blackened world." This book attempts to reconstruct this unfulfilled engagement.[16]

Adorno's response to jazz must be accessed by way of acknowledgment of his anxiety over the fact that individuals are powerless and socially impoverished and that this situation has been exacerbated by the culture industry and its products. The individual holds a problematic but central position in jazz narratives. The term *individual*, which in its most common usage leads us to the image of the defunct bourgeois subject of earlier and less malignant permutations of capitalism, has largely escaped interrogation within jazz studies. Its use has assisted the desire to bring jazz closer to the model provided by Western European concert music and the singularity of the composer and her or his composition. It is an abstraction that leads to the fetishization of the solo as the essence of jazz work. Yet the idea, which finds its (broken) voice with Louis Armstrong's twelve-second introduction on "West End Blues," is considered significant within the most improbable of contexts. The Association for the Advancement of Creative Musicians (AACM) is by many accounts the most successful example of artistic collectivism in black American music. During the fifty years of its activity, it has maintained its commitment to community engagement, collaborative creative work, and the pooling of economic support and resources.[17] During a 2014 panel discussion, cofounder Muhal Richard Abrams stated in no uncertain terms that the AACM is grounded in the contribution of distinct personalities and that "individualism" is a fundamental facet of human existence. It is essential to pay close attention to what Abrams says here, thrown as it is into sharp relief against the communitarianism for which the organization is renowned. I repeat his actual words for clarity: "I realized very early in life . . . I noticed . . . very early in life that individualism was one of the basic [traits of] . . . human nature. Why is it that none of us are alike? Why? . . . So it occurred to me that individualism, being that extensive, meant that all the information was not put in one place. . . . So, I decided that, well, we learn from each other, because he's not like me and I'm not like him, so he'll do something and I'll say, 'Oh you can do it that way,' and vice versa."[18] Abrams's individual is encoded with heterogeneity and distinction. True individualism cannot occur in isolation. It is not captured by mere tolerance of difference. In fact, it goes beyond a virtuous embrace of the best examples of multiculturalism. It involves an awareness of the individual's dependence on what it is not. An individual cannot reach truth alone, "the information" being distributed across each and every one. Or, as Adorno has it, "the concept of freedom does not lie in the isolated subject, but can be grasped only in relation to the constitution of mankind as a whole. Freedom truly consists only in the realization of humanity as such."[19]

Prior to Abrams's having pinpointed it for me, I had taken Adorno's dismissal of the music as pseudo-individualism to be an attack on jazz (supposedly) leading people to believe that the category of the individual still had relevance. I now consider the disparagement to also refer to the debasement of the term itself: the "individual" being defined over and *against* the collective—even as real-life human beings struggle to assert a modicum of personal sovereignty—rather than as existing in empathetic, ceaselessly mutating relations with other individuals and the collective whole. Abrams's nuanced, very particular understanding of individualism helps us to see what is lost in shorthanded parlance. When Adorno tells us it is no longer correct to speak of the individual, he is referring, at least in part, to the fact that the milieu is not conducive to a communal individualism. Faced with the isolation and self-interest propagated by ideology under the cover of which the dehumanizing infrastructure of capitalism and acute rationalization operate, genuine communion retreats into artistic practice, social theory, and those underground spaces that have been rejected or ignored by the societal mainstream. An interest in jazz as representative of this subterranean space, where alternative forms of subjectivity are able to flourish, fuels this study.

What Jazz?

In "Exploding the Narrative in Jazz Improvisation" Vijay Iyer disputes the idea that jazz work "unfold[s] merely in the overall form of a 'coherent' solo" or "simply in antiphonal structures." He urges us to look to "the microscopic musical details" and "the inherent structure of the performance itself." And perhaps most crucial for this book, he stresses that the "story dwells not just in one solo at a time, but also in a single note, and equally in an entire lifetime of improvisations. In short, the story is revealed not as a simple linear narrative, but as a fractured, exploded one."[20] The proposal to contract the focus to minute constructive detail and broaden to a multitude of layers that make up the "lifetime of improvisations" allows for—in fact, calls for—expanded senses of both the loci of jazz work and the kinds of interaction that take place there. Sites of significance in jazz are found not only within the framework provided by the individual improviser, or the real-time interaction of a band, but also within various and combining expressive registers and ensemble configurations. The gatherings of contribution—what Stephen Henderson has termed "massive concentration[s] of Black experiential energy," or "mascons," in his writing on black poetics—frustrate the notion of time- and space-limited collaboration we most often encounter in jazz studies.[21] These intergenerational works represent a markedly different version of the story from the abstract solo of traditional analysis. In this book jazz is shown to be a congregation of musical play in the broadest sense. Crucial groundwork to this alternative analytic is an appreciation of the generative tension between a musician holding on to his or her distinctive characteristics and approach and the commitment to sharing (in) that common story of deviance. The playful tension involved in retelling a communal work in his or her own voice and within his or her own communicative capabilities is the prime site of creative activity. A negotiation of the desire to share in the tradition and the imperative to remain distinct is where the work of a jazz musician is centered. This mimetic attitude is a feature of all artistic pursuit, but it comes into sharp focus when considering jazz. The mimetic negotiations in jazz and other collaborative practices may also be their "unity-constitutive" moments.

Within this understanding of jazz, sociomusical alliances are as likely to occur between Ethel Waters's 1928 interpretation of "West End Blues" and saxophonist Sahib Shihab's contribution on "Monk's Mood" some twenty years later, as they are to be found within one of Miles Davis's venerated quintets.[22] A heterophonic chorus in revolution around the word *mine* and a "multi-stereophonic schmear" created by listening to five versions of Louis Armstrong performing "(What Did I Do to Be So) Black and Blue?" are valid examples of jazz work.[23] The fact that this approach makes the listener-analyst a (poor) collaborator cannot be ignored. The illusion of academic objectivity and invisible authority is forfeited, so perhaps, by customary standards, it is an approach certain to fail. With this caveat in mind I respond in this book to an urgency to meet the music partway. The limited music analysis that is included should be considered tentative probes for more substantial deliberations to come.

The book is written on the assumption that jazz is black music, yet the discussions contained herein help transform that supposition into a well-grounded thesis—a welcome by-product rather than the fruits of any dedicated rumination. My focus is in no way an attempt to define who is able to contribute to jazz, and I am not concerned with adjudication on the "truthfulness" or authenticity of work by nonblack people. I am, however, guided by an interest in approaching the music from an alternative vantage point. It is implied herein that jazz performance (whoever its players may be) is facilitated by the disconnect between black life and its denigration. The book asserts that jazz emerged by way of a mode of subjectivity that allows little respite from self-reflection and one necessarily at play with the way it has been appropriated by, and presented in, society. The principles of structuration in jazz pertain to black life, even in work where "content" does not. That is to say that jazz work, as such, is facilitated by life that is often lived in, but always *is* an embodiment of, critical reflection on the integrity of the world. My exploration of the critical potential of jazz is carried out through the eyes of those who live black life, but it should be made clear from the outset that any insight garnered by such an approach is of consequence to all. In this I am emboldened by Aimé Césaire, who writes: "I'm not going to confine myself to some narrow particularism. But I do not intend either to become lost in a disembodied universalism. . . . I have a different idea of a universal. It is a universal rich with all that is particular, rich with all the particulars there are, the deepening of each particular, the coexistence of them all."[24]

CHAPTER 1

JAZZ, INDIVIDUALISM, AND THE BLACK MODERN

In Mississippi, 1955, after reportedly flirting with a white woman, fourteen-year-old Emmett Till was lynched. Through her refusal to mask the disfigured face of her murdered son, Mamie Bradley brought to the fore of American national consciousness the enduring problem of black dehumanization. All of Till's features had been removed or obscured by the attack and the three days he had spent tied to a cotton gin in the Tallahatchie River. In what were the opening stages of the civil rights era, the brutality visited on this adolescent touched a nerve in a way similar injustices had failed to a decade before. It is telling that in their exploration of the case, Davis Houck and Matthew Grind speak of how the publication in the press of a "holiday picture" was seen at the time as helping to "humaniz[e] the Tills."[1] The word leaps from the page, taking on much more meaning than the authors intended. Humanize. The defense counsel parlance strains under the weight of the particulars of the case, the disfigurement readers are forced to contemplate, and, of course, the history of New World enslavement. In contrast to Till's wolf whistle—the alleged trigger of the attack—the smiling geniality of the holiday photo is a sanctioned mode of black expression. The scandal of that brazen-faced masculinity is corrected by an artless smile in its Sunday best. Bradley's act of disclosure showed the ideology behind such facades of congeniality. The surrender of humanity required of black excursion into social spaces is captured in the image of a corpse that lacks a death mask, an absence reflecting the "afterlife" of slavery. The unyielding impossibility of expressing the horror it had experienced made the nonface a symbol of the ill-fated birth of a community. Till's death is an emblem of the predicament born of mass dehumanization that is the heart of black modernity and the expression to which it gives rise.

∘ ∘ ∘

There is a moment in Theodor Adorno's infamous essay "On Jazz" that forces me to reconsider my dismissal of it as an ignorant impertinence—an unfortunate smell that has me holding my nose as I devour less problematic areas of the theorist's rich corpus. That the principles of structuration in jazz work exceeded his understanding is undeniable. More damning is his near-silence on African American and, more generally, black sociohistory. This is excruciating. Yet a claim made in passing hints at an inadvertent insight into a more faithful (and perhaps, more fruitful) rendition of the relation of blackness to the mainstream: "Perhaps, oppressed peoples could be said to be especially well-prepared for jazz. To some extent, they demonstrate for the not yet adequately mutilated liberals the mechanism of identification with their own oppression."[2] On the face of it the predicament of New World slavery appears to play out in advance the alienation and neutering of the bourgeois subject of the most recent past century and a half. Of course, the relation is closer to metaphor than historical preview. And on further reflection the metaphor is a bad one, as the relation between blackness and the human is often one of disjunctive intimacy. At a minor second interval from one another, they are discordant and too close to be effective allegory. Adorno's preoccupation with the individual belongs to an intellectual "history that excludes [black people] . . . from even the shared experience of fragmentation."[3]

It is both a testament to the persuasion of the ideology of individuality and damning evidence of the poor standing of black discontent within scholarly discourse that literature on jazz has tended to assume it to be in service of that "shared experience of fragmentation" from which black America and its colonial compatriots are routinely barred. Commentators throughout its history have seen jazz as music of the individual. It has been portrayed as a conduit of unhampered human essence and as a mirror of an idealized democratic society. But for Adorno, in the context of the actual isolation and lack of freedom that individuals encounter in modern life, this acclaim leaves the music open to the charges of complicity and regression. If we accept these accounts from jazz commentary, then we also need to take seriously Adorno's objections concerning the music. But I do not believe these are the only or the most pertinent narratives. The insufficient engagement from the vantage of black subjectivity in jazz commentary is a lack that Adorno takes on without reflection. The omission undermines his critique. If an inquiry into how "the individual" features within this community in light of a history of systematic dehumanization had been made, Adorno would have found that black expression cannot be understood solely (or primarily) against the backdrop of the tragedy of the bourgeoisie. African American expression is neither an affirmation of personal autonomy nor a reluctance to relinquish a faded and now-defunct social category of a bygone era. Rather, it is a facet of a life that cannot help but be a critical reflection on the integrity of the world.

The Embattled Individual of the "Old Bourgeoisie"

Adorno's concern over individuals' loss of autonomy in the era of monopolistic capitalism impels his efforts to expose the unscrupulous underbelly of the culture industry. In *Minima Moralia: Reflections on a Damaged Life*—which reads as part autopsy, part eyewitness testimony chronicling the demise of the "old bourgeois class"—Adorno tells us of the brave new world in which "each statement, each piece of news, each thought has been pre-formed by the centres of the culture industry. Whatever lacks the familiar trace of such pre-formation lacks credibility."[4] This is clearly a milieu hostile to independent, unsolicited intervention of socially engaged individuals. At the height of bourgeois liberalism the family was the primary source of values for an individual. "Ego-autonomy," which was nurtured within the patriarchal setting, held the possibility of individuals developing alternative ways of living and relating to others. The resolved Oedipus complex shows the emergent ego of an individual to conform in large part with the values and opinions that it spent some of its formative period reacting against. The rebellion involved in this development is crucial, however, to securing the tools necessary for effective agitation of societal values at risk of entrenchment.

With the growth of monopolizing business and corporations, and the accompanying power exercised by the state, this freedom became increasingly tenuous. The economic autonomy that the bourgeoisie had under market capitalism dissipates, undermining its stewardship over the ego development of the nascent generation. In the new "fatherless" society the collective psyche is primed for manipulation. The ill-formed ego provides little resistance to the culture industry. The decline of the bourgeoisie that is linked to the rise of the new anonymous order, in which capital becomes increasingly centralized, renders class division redundant. In this precarious environment, in which the family has lost its role as protector, a beleaguered universal class welcomes the reawakening of its underattended superego—fascist despots and the culture industry supplant the patriarch, who no longer possesses the necessary moral authority.[5] As György Márkus tells it, "The culture industry largely takes over the function of the socialization of individuals, imbuing them at all levels of their psychological constitution with common patterns of reality-interpretation and behavior, making them thereby unresisting executers of the required functions of an encompassing system of impersonal domination." He continues, quoting Adorno: "It is 'the social cement,' 'the glue which still keeps together commodity society today, after it has already been condemned economically.' For 'the need that might have somehow resisted central control is already repressed by the control of individual consciousness.'"[6]

The compulsion to conform is in direct conflict with the ability to become an individual and nurture empathetic relationships with others. In "Freudian Theory and the Pattern of Fascist Propaganda" Adorno sketches a situation in which followers identify with "an omnipotent and unbridled father figure, by far transcending the individual father and therewith apt to be enlarged into a 'group ego.'"[7] Hostility toward minority groups is one consequence of this, and by the very fact of being part of the "group ego," the follower is superior to those who are not. A person values him- or herself to the extent that he or she is a member of the group that grants admittance only to those who buy into the fiction of that group's superiority. Any "interaction" is shown to be in service of the dominating forces, which punish nonconformity with expulsion from the "in-group." In these more recent permutations of capitalism, "people are really atomized and separated from each other by an unbridgeable chasm," and their interaction "issue[s] neither from their free will nor from their instincts but from social and economic laws which prevail over their heads."[8] This is the background against which we must read Adorno's encounter with jazz.

"Jazz Is America"—Individualism and Liberty in Jazz Commentary

Jazz is often presented as music of the individual.[9] Its improvisational character is given as evidence of the independence of its musicians. It is also hailed as the bearer of a democratic spirit that is manifest in its inclusiveness, its musical miscegenation, and its rejection of the composer-performer division of labor we find in the modern European tradition. Moreover, its spirit of spontaneity, and what appears as an unadulterated expression of life, acts as an antidote to the self-alienation experienced in most other areas of modern existence. Narratives of the individual have featured in jazz studies from early in its history. The proto–jazz studies contributions of Hugues Panassié and Robert Goffin—contemporaries of Adorno—present the notion that jazz was a remedy to the degradation inflicted on people by capitalism and the acute rationalization underpinning that malevolent system.

Alongside, and often interlaced with, the undeniably astute critical insight was a quasi-religious enthusiasm that, at times, revealed casual racism.[10] Goffin in 1934, with particular evangelical fervor, enthuses: "Oh you musicians of my life, prophets of my youth, splendid Negroes informed with fire, how shall I ever express my love for your saxophones writhing like orchids, your blazing trombones with their hairpin vents, your voices fragrant with all the breezes of home remembered and the breath of the bayous, your rhythm as inexorable as tom-toms beating in an African nostalgia!"[11] There can be little doubt that such writing fed into established imagery and imaginings that keep black heterogeneity manageably narrow. The portrayal of musicians such as Louis Armstrong as "simple, naive [and] jovial" mediums who were mere physicality—sweating like heavyweights and "foam[ing] at the mouth" while waving a white handkerchief of surrender/submission—strays too close to "Sambo," the perennial of minstrelsy and a category that helps govern black incursions into mainstream space.[12] So it is with caution that I argue that Panassié and Goffin's encounter with jazz needs to be retraced beyond the veneer of "noble savage" racism to their belief that the music had the potential to reawaken human qualities degraded by the unchecked rationalization of life.

Jazz, interpreted as a manifestation of freedom from intellectualized approaches to creative expression, is understood by the primitivists to come from a people with direct access to a primal human essence all but lost by their European counterparts. Rather than the insidious calculation of the tradition with which these writers are most familiar, jazz represents an alternative, drawing from resources that evade the suffusive instrumentality of human capability. Jazz musicians were viewed by these scholars as conduits to a reservoir of the "spontaneous urge of a whole people."[13] Revered as a prophet, the jazz musician was called on to demonstrate to the European modern a means of escaping the perils of civilization and of reuniting with its essential being. Panassié and others of this school were driven by a desire to turn from Western society's hothouse rationality and its scientification of life toward a more elemental state. In their writing, jazz appears abstracted from a black sociohistorical context to serve the needs of a spiritually bankrupt European bourgeoisie. Their at times quasi-evangelical tracts offered this audience a particular response to a bourgeois predicament and had little, if anything, to do with a black experience of modernity. For the primitivists, jazz represented a route of return to a pre-Enlightenment European sensibility.

○ ○ ○

The enduring narrative of individuality in jazz sees the music as the mirror of an idealized American society—one founded on the sovereignty of the individual but respectful of the need for concessions that allow for a pragmatic democracy. Indeed, bolstered by the fact of its black origins, jazz was weaponized by the State Department to play a significant role in the promotion of the United States as the foremost proprietor of human rights. On the Cold War–era international radio show *Voice of America Jazz Hour*, Willis Conover impressed on his listeners the democratic foundations of jazz: "Only in such a society—and ours is the best example I know—could jazz have developed. It has its own musical restrictions—tempo, key, chord structure. But within them the artist is free to weave infinite variations. Structurally, it's a democratic music. People from other countries, in other political situation[s], detect this element of freedom in jazz. There isn't any elaborate reasoning process involved. They can feel it—emotionally. They love jazz because they love freedom."[14]

In a similar vein, more recently, critic Gary Giddins writes, with arresting conviction: "The one truth about jazz of which I am certain is that it incarnates liberty, often with a perversely proud intransigence, merging with everything and borrowing anything, yet ultimately riding alone."[15] In such accounts jazz is presented as an expressive form founded on an ethos of tolerance, synthesizing difference into a cohesive whole but somehow managing to "ultimately rid[e] alone." The music solves the conundrum of how to go about encouraging self-reliance while supporting the communitarianism necessary for a functioning democratic society. In contrast to primitivists' staging of jazz as redemptive—a conduit to a prerational, intuitive essence—the dominant portrait of individualism in jazz shows the music to be reflective of American liberal democracy.[16] For the primitivist, jazz presented a course of spiritualized action, a way that decadent modern Europeans, through immersion in the experience of a jazz performance, could be cleansed. Jazz-as-democracy employs the music as evidence of American moral superiority.

For John A. Kouwenhoven, in jazz "the thing that holds [musicians] together is the thing they are all so busy flouting: the fundamental four-four beat."[17] The music is at its best when "each player seems to be—and has the sense of being—on his own. Each goes his own way, inventing rhythmic and melodic patterns that, superficially, seem to have . . . little relevance to one another . . . yet the outcome is a dazzlingly precise creative unity. . . . Jazz is the first art form to give full expression to [Ralph Waldo] Emerson's ideal of a union which is perfect only 'when all the uniters are isolated.' "[18] In a similar vein Ralph Ellison understood genuine jazz to be "an art of individual assertion within and against the group. Each true jazz moment (as distinct from the uninspired commercial performance) springs from a contest in which each artist challenges all the rest; each solo flight, or improvisation, represents (like the successive canvases of a painter) a definition of his identity as individual, as member of the collectivity and as a link in the chain of tradition."[19] This description of the music speaks to a tension at the heart of the United States' founding documents—the crux of the ideal of America: how to maintain a common good while encouraging the self-reliance of a nation of individuals. Yet black America, while contributing to "democratic symbolic action," by way of its expression in jazz, poses a direct challenge to the understanding of the terms *America*, *freedom*, and *democracy*. For Emerson the situation of the black modern exemplified how these terms had come to represent a reality diametrically opposed to them.[20] He poured scorn on the interpretative contortions that proslavery advocates performed in order to uphold the Declaration of Independence *and* retain the institution of slavery.[21]

Ellison, perhaps more essentially, draws attention to the seeming incongruity of being black and human/individual. He laments that the black American, "a most complex example of Western man," is most often drawn in mainstream representations as an "oversimplified clown." The complexities and contradictions that make for compelling characterization are denied. The very idea of a black man or woman embodying "complexity and minuteness of differentiations" (Dewey) poses a challenge to the conventional truths that structure and continue to uphold modern society.[22] What is most striking here is the contradiction between black expression (jazz) being a bearer of the liberal democratic ideal and black life being considered devoid of human quality. Within the general social field, black humanity is an aberration, a contradiction in terms. And genuine expression emerging from such life—particularly a practice hinged on idiosyncratic, distinctive response, such as jazz—should not be possible. This contradiction is not an irregularity but rather a peculiarity of black (American) subject formation.

Anticipating discussions that will follow in subsequent chapters, I suggest here that jazz cannot be adequately understood through a reading that sees the individual soloist fully liberated within the confines of predetermined rules and expectations nor through one that portrays a group of "isolated" individuals who merely inhabit the same space and miraculously turn out "coherent" work. The democracy narrative recognizes a collective in jazz but misconstrues the complex, contradictory, irresolvable relationships as a harmonious resolution to do what one wants, so long as one is tolerant. Kouwenhoven and Giddins are as deaf to the clanging contradictions of coupling jazz with liberty as elected upholders of the Constitution were as they voted in the Fugitive Slave Act. It is this persistent theme in jazz commentary concerning the reconciliation of a supposedly free individual and a benevolent society that Adorno finds so hard to swallow. To be clear: it is not the fact that jazz insufficiently models individual freedom that bothers Adorno. Rather, what troubles him is, as he sees it, parasitic propaganda asserting that such self-determination is a possibility in modern/contemporary life.

The Jazz Critique

These claims made on behalf of jazz are the source of Adorno's misgivings concerning the music. The idea that jazz "provides a metaphorical solution" to the crisis of the modern human, that it is able to "encourage individuality without selfishness and . . . civic mindedness without totalitarianism" is a fallacy.[23] It is not just a harmless fiction; it is ideology in service to that against which it feigns rebellion. Adorno wants us to view the music as but a tool of coercion and control. Lack of formal necessity, in which phrases, sections, and whole choruses of solos can be rearranged at will in the absence of any sense of internal logic, is thought to betray this ulterior purpose. If jazz is allowed any musical significance, that significance occurs at its surface, within properties ordinarily considered subordinate to the structuring harmonic and thematic movements of a piece. The music is organized to effortlessly produce the appearance of novelty time and again, recycling structural formulas *ad infinitum*.[24] "The elements in jazz in which immediacy seems to be present," Adorno writes, "the seemingly improvisational moments—of which syncopation is designated as its elemental form—are added in their naked externality to the standardized commodity character in order to mask it—without, however, gaining power over it for a second."[25] Formal principles allow for ease of production, marketing, and reception. Jazz is a commodity in a strict sense. In opposition to most popular interpretations, the music, for Adorno, is inextricably shackled to the demands of the market; thus, it cannot hope to achieve the critical distance necessary for independent development.

Jazz is hollow under the eggshell-thin surface of its "subjective expression," toward which improvisation and its rudimental descendant, syncopation, are considered prominent tools. That which is presented as "revolt against a collective power"[26] is in fact an ever-replenishing supply of disposable veneers that mask the music's compliance with the dominating structure: "He who is reproducing the music is permitted to tug at the chains of his boredom, and even to clatter them, but he cannot break them."[27] Marketed as spontaneity and innovation, it in fact betrays an adherence to a law of the market that calls for work to "constantly remain the same while at the same time constantly simulating the 'new,'" a demand that "cripples all productive power."[28] Concomitantly, jazz forges counterfeit identities at a time when the individual has all but surrendered a means of response. It fabricates reconciliation between the individual and society in an attempt to conceal mass atomization and the breaking down of difference into blanket categories. Works that are genuinely progressive do not attempt to gloss over these contradictions of modern living. Jazz not only makes light of these insurmountable challenges to personal autonomy; it resides, opportunistically, in their grooves.

It is hard not to be frustrated by Adorno's Eurocentrism; his cultural allegiances work through the jazz essays in the negative. Theodore Gracyk points out that a "jazz [work] is misunderstood when viewed only as a composition."[29] The extent of Adorno's guilt on this point is debatable—he clearly recognizes the centrality of improvisation—but there is no denying that he views jazz through a lens that sees composition as the predominant site of artistry. What is perhaps more interesting in this exchange is that Gracyk completes the sentence quoted above by dissenting that jazz's "emphasis is on individuality and individual performance," holding up these qualities as evidence of worth without recognizing that such an admission points to a more penetrating, and more difficult, conversation with Adorno than he affords. Gracyk glosses Adorno's concerns regarding the individual and jazz by confining the issue to an extensive use of "standards." Not only does this fail to factor in the broader and more complex picture of black access to American ideals; it ignores (or at least fails to recognize) the critical context of Adorno's rejection of the possibility of individuality in late capitalist society. In his desire to show jazz to be music of the individual, Gracyk adds weight to the charge that the music is ideological. Attempting to unshackle jazz from popular song, that which he considered the culpable party, Gracyk undermines the importance of polyvocality (the centrality of the standard or of common nodes of musical and cultural significance) to jazz and its undeniable heteronomous nature. The positing of jazz as a music of the individual, often in quixotic harmony with the collective, only confirms what Adorno believes is troubling about it.[30] Adorno's argument on this point is compelling. He highlights how jazz is erroneously presented as a solution to the problem of how we can be individualistic without causing harm to others. He casts doubt on claims that jazz embodies a version of communalistic living that avoids prejudice. If jazz presents itself as an embodiment of the individual in an age in which that mode of subjectivity has become impossible to maintain, then it must be propaganda in the service of society's repressive forces.

My discussion of primitivist jazz commentary and Emersonian liberalism should make clear that this narrative of the embattled individual is not an Adornian quirk. Rather, it is a key theme of critical theory and a preoccupation of European and Euro-American humanities more broadly, one that resounds in the present. To be sure, our collective lack of freedom reveals itself at every strata of social life—with a stranglehold on the private, too. It is manifest in the restrictions on the manner in which we are to keep ourselves alive: the necessity of work, and work of a certain kind; the malevolent paternalism of personal banking; our consumption being appropriated and controlled by markets over which we have virtually no control; and the bombardment of images (and their encoded messages) we are almost continually fed, through both traditional and new media. For Adorno it is the lived reality of ever-increasing isolation and the petering-out of self-determination that discredits the image of jazz as liberation. How can the music speak in such triumphant tones when faced with the facts of wholesale alienation and degradation? This is what Adorno finds so objectionable. The jazz musician as redeemer, spinning off-the-cuff musical retorts in opposition to the rigidity of the popular song forms, is misleading; the opposition is a straw man, the musician being wholly dependent on that which he critically reworks. In fact, he reaffirms, through the reiteration of the individuality myth, his allegiance to the establishment.

Adorno argues that, despite claims to the contrary, the "jazz subject" is not free but is implicated in an activity that renders the successful resolution of the Oedipus complex both unnecessary and undesirable. Under the inauspicious conditions of late capitalism, the formation of the bourgeois ego is perfectly adapted to one pertaining to a new "universal class," as full advantage is taken of its lack of self-determination. The redundant process of super-ego internalization becomes an unquestioning identification with the surrogate father figure—in this case the culture industry. But this identity, which masquerades in jazz as perpetually repeating acts of rebellion, has no intention of transcending the mock conflict. In fact, "by learning to fear social authority and experiencing it as a threat of castration—and immediately as fear of impotence—it identifies itself with precisely this authority of which it is afraid."[31] The eventual overcoming of the fear of castration that results in novel outlooks being found by emergent individuals—albeit in "consultation" with family values—and that have in the past equipped them with vital tools of resistance, is now deferred indefinitely. The jazz subject, as part of a new, universal consumer class, is able to take part in totalitarian society in exchange for her or his ability to develop genuine subjecthood.

The jazz musician, or "hot subject," demonstrates to the consumer how to go about identifying with the dominating forces in society.[32] He does this through the use in his music of syncopation and "breaks" (short, improvised sections), which are meant to suggest transcendence of the authority of the form but, in fact, are not only inextricably attached to the structure of the composition but also interchangeable with it. Adorno tells us that the "jazz subject . . . falls out of the collective just as syncopation does from the regular beat; it does not want to be engulfed in the prescribed majority, which existed before the subject and is independent of it, whether out of protest or ineptitude or both at once—until it finally is received into, or, better, subordinated to the collective as it was predestined to do; until the music indicates . . . that it was a part of it from the very beginning; that, itself a part of this society, it can never really break away from it." Adorno argues that jazz models for the "not yet adequately mutilated liberals" how to go about making adjustments so that they fit the dominant social rhythm of the day while feigning disdain for that authority. Adorno believes, in fact, that in jazz there is an acknowledgment of this contradiction. Its posturing as individuality and "superiority" over the collective is not to be taken completely seriously: "the playful superiority of the individual over society, which precisely because of its exact knowledge of the rules of its game can dare not to strictly maintain them."[33] Compounding the societal changes that restrict the development of authentic relationships is the baggage accompanying the weakened ego. With the replacement of originality and independent thought with mass conformity—at times masquerading as individuality—the nurturing of difference that makes for productive, empathetic relationships is undermined. The much-lauded balance between the individual and the collective in the jazz band is exposed as false. Jazz's supposed democratic character is seen as an impossibility within a society of atomized subjects. In fact, jazz is not a mere victim of these tendencies but is an accomplice, "imped[ing] the development of autonomous, independent individuals who judge and decide consciously for themselves."[34] For Adorno the fact is that "people are really atomized and separated from each other by an unbridgeable chasm,"[35] and in claiming otherwise, jazz is guilty of perpetuating the myth of individualism that accompanies and attempts to mask the "totally administered society."

Yet one is left with a bothersome question: is it really possible to mount an effective evaluation of jazz's complicity without understanding the very particular relation black life has to America, democracy, and liberty? Among his defenders there is a tendency to naturalize rather than challenge Adorno's unflinching but largely unreflective focus on the bourgeoisie in his address of jazz. It is indicative of a more general silence. For instance, it would seem most unlikely but is nonetheless true that no attempt has been made to correct the disingenuity of Adorno's defensive claim made during his 1953 exchange on jazz with Joachim-Ernst Berendt to being "largely responsible for the most widely discussed American book about an understanding of race prejudice."[36] *The Authoritarian Personality*, despite exploring out-group prejudice in the United States, fails to include even a cursory examination of racism suffered by African Americans.

Adorno and the Black Modern

Adorno overestimates the ability of the bourgeois narrative to provide a comprehensive survey of the problems that beset individuals and their relationships in modernity. The largely unreflective positing of this nominated representative—whom Adorno considers the most advanced consciousness of the late capitalist period—as the catchall and executor of all other subjectivities leaves something wanting in his consideration of jazz.[37] For the uninitiated, Adorno's very specific tailoring of Marxist thought, particularly his devaluation of the critical and revolutionary potential of proletarian consciousness, spliced with, again, a characteristically idiosyncratic reading of Freud, on which this centrality of the bourgeois as the main subject of modernity is supported, seems a little parochial. In *Minima Moralia* Adorno speaks of the situation of the bourgeoisie in late capitalism as one of a lingering power in decline. In his rejection of the prospect of an enlightened working class, he in turn lingers on the bourgeoisie as the defining consciousness of the era. Despite what his tone often betrays, however, this focus is more than a personal, nostalgic response to the decline of the class with which he identifies.

In his book *Adorno's Aesthetics of Music* Max Paddison draws from Michael de la Fontaine's defense of this focus on the bourgeoisie and its "art music." Adorno believes there is no longer a distinct class that produces folk music, "whose songs and games could be taken up and sublimated by art."[38] He maintains that in late capitalism there are no longer independent classes and thus no genuine expression to speak of. Rather than the "vitality" of folk forms infusing and rejuvenating "art music," we are faced with a situation in which corrupted forms are "controlled 'from above' by the historically 'obsolete and devalued materials of art music.' "[39] This historical offering is bolstered by a theoretical one that tells us "the bourgeois individual is the Subject/Object which, in the form of rationality, can be seen as representing in its purest form the socially necessary degree of domination and control. . . . The proletarian individual . . . is regarded as *the socially derived Object*, carrying socially superfluous domination within itself."[40] In Adorno's jazz essays the limitations of this narrow conception of subjectivity-as-bourgeois are brought into relief, and these shortcomings are shown to be of consequence not only for understanding jazz and its black subject but, perhaps most important, for mining all possibilities for critical responses to the pervasive effects of monopolistic capitalism. Driven by a comparable concern for the absence of the proletariat in Adorno, Jamie Owen Daniel writes that "the bourgeois modality of subjectivity, the 'individual,' is not the only available subjective mode, and that a different and competing working-class mode has existed, but has been representationally suppressed, not least of all in the modernist cultural production that Adorno privileges."[41] The assumption in Adorno that all other "modes" of subjectivities are subordinate—"socially derived" from the "most advanced" consciousness of the day—assumes, at best, that the bourgeois condition is taken on by all. But under interrogation it also points to the proposition that those alternative modes are inessential to a full appreciation of the cataclysmic trajectory taken by capitalism and the accompanying rationalization of life.

The black experience does not figure into Adorno's jazz critique. In "Über Jazz," first published in 1936, the African American basis of jazz is all but denied. He writes: "The extent to which jazz has anything at all to do with genuine black music is highly questionable; the fact that it is frequently performed by blacks and that the public clamors for 'black jazz' as a sort of brand-name doesn't say much about it, even if folkloric research should confirm the African origin of many of its practices."[42] Where in later work Adorno accepts the "folkloric research" that places jazz history squarely within the black community, he reprimands the music for failing to retain elements of "unruliness." If it were the case that a more genuine expression had not been corrupted "from above," then there might be something worth considering for critical potential. In "Perennial Fashion—Jazz" (1953) he writes, "However little doubt there can be regarding the African elements in jazz, it is no less certain that everything unruly in it was from the very beginning integrated into a strict scheme, that its rebellious gestures are accompanied by the tendency to blind obeisance."[43]

This rare reference to African America reinforces Adorno's dismissal of any possibility that its expressive forms have the potential to present a sufficient challenge. In provocation he asserts that a music that has roots in "Negro spirituals" and "slave songs," with their "lament of unfreedom [combined] with its oppressed confirmation," could not possibly nurture practitioners able to develop autonomous responses to their subordination.[44] In a similar vein he writes, with regard to the inability of the proletariat to furnish distinctive, independent music forms, "the realism taught by want is not as one with the free unfoldment of consciousness."[45] And surely this would have been applied to the African American, too, had the connection between experience and consciousness been deemed more tenable. Save the passage from "Perennial Fashion—Jazz" quoted above, an African American perspective is not so much written into the periphery of Adorno's narrative of modernity as placed outside it. It is safe to assume that Adorno considered the black experience wholly inconsequential to the narrative of the modern on which his culture critique rested. Jazz, however, in its portrayal as pure commodity, was integral, and this is due, in part, to its perceived lack of musical history or tradition. As a marketing tool—as "coloristic effect" and brand development—the "hot musician" was considered to have an indispensable function in the culture industry. But in his writing we find Adorno uses black life in a comparable way. We find reified fragments of poorly formed ideas, bordering on caricature, which add false depth to Adorno's jazz critique. There is an implication that the modern black has, in a sense, previewed, under a distinct set of circumstances, the disenfranchisement of the bourgeoisie under monopolistic capitalism. Adorno invites us to read jazz as a fable through which we can grasp the predicaments of bourgeois subjectivity a little better. The provocation of remarks such as a portrayal of jazz as "housebroken and scrubbed behind the ears," or of the jazz subject from whom he hears "I am nothing, I am filth, no matter what they do to me, it serves me right," serve mainly in a metaphorical capacity; but they stray much too close to, without ever acknowledging or addressing, certain psychological repercussions of chattel slavery.[46]

Yet one can do better than dismiss this as mere Eurocentric ignorance. To cite Fred Moten, there is a certain "insight Adorno's deafness carries."[47] It is hard to believe that Adorno made the allusions to slavery and black subordination without awareness of the connotations they evoked. After all, Adorno was anything but disarming. His shock-jock rhetorical devices were not limited to the jazz essays. They are employed with an upending effect throughout his corpus. But while Adorno scripted black burlesque for allegoric use in presenting the experience of the new "universal class" or the "jazz subject," the careless glance cast over the psychological trauma of black America invites us to inquire into this history to which he has paid the scantest of attention. Ironically, through this we are able to challenge his characterization of jazz as complicit in culture industry manipulation and to set the groundwork for discussions to come concerning the critical potential of jazz.

In place of the myth of individualism, behind which bourgeois degradation occurs, we find the black/slave systematically stripped of any trace of self-determination and without ideology to mask the fact.[48] Indeed, the overt nature of black subjugation is an integral part of this regulation, a counterpart to hoodwinking pseudo-individualism that performs to control the middle classes. The subordination of both subjectivities is facilitated by a bleeding-out of difference—as strategies to further the efficacious commodification of human beings and to create a pool of pliable consumer labor. Crucially, however, the enslaved required no accompanying ideas of illusory self-determination. In fact, slaves were supplied with a steady flow of justification for their enslavement, the fact of their subordination pronounced to them regularly and unequivocally.[49] While Adorno's pseudo-individual is coached toward recognizing the fascist leader as a partial reflection of herself and is thus led to believe in an alleged self-sovereignty, the black person must address head-on the fact of her weakness and is encouraged to see herself as nothing but a marker of "race."[50] The point bears repeating. The ideology of individualism, of democratized sovereignty, which allows the system of *universal* domination to continue unabated, is not extended to black people. Black life can have no stake in the world and so is not party to the modes of deception that accompany the privilege. It is also clear that whatever of their life manages to escape sanctioned and appropriated functions of the mainstream—that is, insofar as they depart from what is presupposed or expected of them—will not show up there.

The reduction of the heterogeneity of life to predetermined categories, and the degradation of African captives to the fungible commodities, sets the context for thinking through "African American culture . . . as a collective enterprise in strict antinomy to the individualistic synthesis of the dominant culture."[51] Through society's collective vision, the phobogenic clod made up of multiple matrices of conceptual and symbolic apparatus is mediated through every black person. This is what Hortense J. Spillers so usefully terms the "mass-in-the-individual." It is also what Frantz Fanon captures as he depicts the unease that his presence generated on the 1950s Parisian boulevard—the inescapable "fact of blackness."[52] The blackness of one's skin obliterates any trace of human particularity, replacing the distinction and singularity—that which marks the human, but not the slave, out from commodity—with a predetermined, one-size-fits-all racial cast. "Every Black Man/Woman *is* the 'race.' " Yet, black life *is* lived, although often invisibly, alongside its appropriated and transformed mainstream uses. Regardless of whether a black person actively embraces "the badge of color" (Du Bois), he or she cannot possibly avoid the need for constant negotiation. That is to say that the play with the disfigurement of his or her life as imaged by the general social field is something of a second nature for black folk. While the significance of sociopolitical commitment in thought and expression should not be diminished, there is a need to assert the fact that black life, whatever the intention of a particular actor, cannot but help be lived *as* critical reflection. I would surmise that this "second sight" is not a choice or a privilege of an enlightened or committed few, but a condition of being black. A black person living in the West and among Westerners (and there are, arguably, few places left in the world that do not, on one register or another, belong to the West), through the ways her everyday living fails to correspond with the image she confronts of herself, will cast doubt on the world's integrity.[53] Moreover, the collective pulling out of, pulling away from, and pulling apart of these categories of control that this everyday living cannot but help perform creates an unstable, ever constellating gathering of difference. The deformation is the work of a congregation of deviance. This is by no means a consolidated, final triumph of the individual or a group of individuals. Rather, it is a union of differentiation—the ground or a model for an attitude or ethics that sees "the thought of the many as no longer inimical."[54] In a significant way, our usual understanding of an autonomous, atomized, private individual must be considered an abstraction in relation to black America. What we see through its eyes is not a yearning for a now defunct category of individual but a disposition to vandalize the categorical smoothness of race, often through passive, uncommitted yet unavoidably critical existence. It is this deviance from mainstream ideals and imaginings, rather than liberty or democracy, that jazz works through.

Hearing "We" When the Singer Says "I"

In a key passage toward the end of "On Jazz" Adorno considers the use of verse-refrain compositional structure in jazz, in an attempt to reiterate a central tenet of his essay—that the "[jazz] subject is not a 'free,' lyrical subject which is then elevated into the collective, but rather one which is not originally free—a victim of the collective."[55] Bypassing what was, by his account, a largely unreliable source of commentary on jazz, Adorno wants to allow the music itself to uphold his speculations concerning its adherence to currents of societal control, and a corresponding lack of personal autonomy. The "jazz subject" is shown to be at best a defenseless dunce duped by the lure of immediacy on tap, and perhaps, more damningly, a sadomasochist, who is aware of the potential harm but who, in exchange for brief moments of gratification, is on hand to help perpetuate the myths that surround her or his manipulation. Adorno contends that this is played out in the verse-refrain form, which he identifies as jazz's compositional structure of choice.[56] The verse-refrain form is most readily recognized as the song structure commonly used in the big production Hollywood musicals of the 1930s and 1940s, in which the verse segues the dialogue into the full-blown song of the chorus. In Adorno's analysis the verse is representative of the individual, who is subordinate to and eventually subsumed into the (often) musically superior chorus, which represents society. The composed verse is often bland, a simple melody that provides ample opportunity for expressive variation when it comes to be performed. For Adorno, however, the performance is not genuine freedom. From the outset the verse, despite the supposedly liberating use of rubato and a skeletal melody that invites fleshing out by the soloist, is secondary. The verse is a "warm-up act" to the chorus, and the soloist's attempts to take what is made to seem like previously untrodden paths out of the unadorned melodic line are illusory. Adorno writes:

> It falls out of the collective just as syncopation does from the regular beat; it does not want to be engulfed in the prescribed majority, which existed before the subject and is independent of it, whether out of protest or ineptitude or both at once—until it finally is received into, or, better, subordinated to the collective as it was predestined to do; until the music indicates, in a subsequently ironic manner as the measures grow rounder, that it was a part of it from the very beginning; that, itself a part of this society, it can never really break away from it.[57]

The individual efforts of the verse are a mere token, an apparent concession to ease the impossibility of genuine individualism. In reality there is no immediacy, no true expression, only a puppet with an eccentric facade who is dedicated to fulfilling the interests of the collective.

The blues "form" cannot be adequately appreciated by recourse to the twelve-bar structure with which we are presented when we attempt to write it up in traditional analysis. Indeed, one might argue that the word *form* and its associated analytical baggage are ill-equipped to excavate this prime site of black American heterophonic expression (what literary critic Stephen Henderson terms "mascon," or "a *massive concentration of Black experiential energy*").[58] It should not come as a surprise—although it often does, approaching the matter from the perspective of the European tradition—that a music inextricably tied to community tends to retreat when faced with attempts to treat it as an autonomous text. We struggle, as Ralph Ellison has it, when we fail to "keep the painful details and episodes of a brutal experience [that of the African American] alive."[59] But even as we put to one side these more qualitative features in an attempt to meet Adorno partway, we can show how the blues form is perhaps a more appropriate structure through which to explore how the individual and the collective relate in the African American experience and in jazz.[60]

The basic twelve-bar variant of the blues starts with a call (a statement, question, accusation) that is repeated (with difference) and then answered by a second theme. The use of antiphony is unexceptional, being a common compositional and performance tool of many genres, including those of the modern European tradition. But the economy—some might argue, the poverty—of the blues form is noteworthy. Its rudimentary nature links it to the verse. Both depend on simplicity of composition. In the verse this tends to be manifested in a throwaway melody; in blues it appears most significantly in its highly formulaic harmonic movement. The lack of musical interest at this compositional level allows for greater contribution by musicians in performance. In fact, as we will see in Chapter 4, the blues intentionally allows for many repetitions and is constituted so as to aid the memorization and dissemination of its compositions. This is where it parts company with the verse, whose components rarely bear much repetition, either in terms of musicality or the ability to be readily committed to memory. As Susan McClary argues, the genius of the blues, which is undeniably "impoverished" (from the standpoint of European harmony), is its ability to facilitate "so many rich and varied repertoires." Its humanity and expression are registered not in its underlying structural harmony, as is typically the case with European artp music, but rather in its unfettered interpretation of the written melody in performance.[61]

Unsurprisingly, the socioaesthetic significance of the blues is lost once we shoehorn it into the mold of Adorno's method, particularly in light of the compositional focus we find in the verse-refrain analysis. To draw out the African American context of the blues, we must look to the profligacy of repetition in the form both within an individual performance and as it manifests itself across numerous interpretations of a piece (both of which suggest something of a temporalized heterophony).[62] John Coltrane contended that the collective is often sounded in the "I."[63] In other words, when he plays, listeners should be able to hear the tradition and the wider social context from which the music emerges. When a work of blues is performed, it sets off constellations of communal associations, ranging from other renderings of the same lyrics or melody to a mixed bag of inflection, riff, and theme, to the kinds of associations that evoke Ellison's more esoteric "jagged grain . . . of a brutal experience."[64] The blues musician is compelled to return to these "mascons," but the repetitions are never self-same; driven by a propensity toward deviance, their responses are always reformations, deformations, and interruptions. The gathering of contribution that makes up a standard is a celebration of aberration. Within this understanding the communal quality of the blues is self-regulating: it belongs to no one, and neither will it congeal around common interests. In attracting a wealth of distinctive contribution and in its establishment of unions of distinction, the blues remains a living, constantly reforming embrace of difference. Perhaps it is the expression of this agitated communal subject—only grasped through a focused consideration of how the individual *cannot* figure in the black community—that continued to confound Adorno in his extended engagement with the music. Perhaps if he had taken the opportunity to tune into the dissonance between everyday black life and how it appears in mainstream imagination, Adorno might have happened on this alternative source of social critique.

CHAPTER 2

DOUBLE CONSCIOUSNESS AND THE CRITICAL POTENTIAL OF BLACK EXPRESSION

According to Adorno, autonomous works of art, by virtue of their peculiar attuned-outsider perspective, are ideally positioned to provide a kind of social critique. Although implicated sociohistorically in the advance of technorationality—in fact, *because* they are so implicated—musical works are able, in rearticulating the pool of available musical material, to expose the poor state of human relations within late capitalist society. Through their fidelity to an expressive tradition, and the internal logic with which musical material is reformed and extended, autonomous works have potential for providing insight into the problems that plague modern living. They are also able to present, through their form, a model of a future noncoercive collectivity. Through form, within the play between discrete aspects and their coming together in the creation of the work, we can glimpse a model of progressive sociality. Jazz is also thought to embody "sedimented" sociohistory, although in *its* case Adorno wants us to focus on how it is distributed and consumed rather than on its formal characteristics, the poverty of which, we are told, is testament to the music's commitment to its affirmative role in consumer society. The principles motivating the creation of jazz works have little to do with artistic expression but rather exist to facilitate works being (re)produced, marketed, and consumed with ease. He writes, "Jazz is a commodity in the strict sense: its suitability for use permeates its production in terms none other than its marketability."[1] It could be argued, and Adorno more or less declares this, that the version of "jazz" on which he is focused is one *appropriated* (that is, extracted and made appropriate) from the African American cultural milieu, in which heterophonia, collaboration, and open-ended play are minimized to draw to the fore values in keeping with mainstream sensibility. If we, contra Adorno, retain or attempt to recover what is not captured—that which evades and that which is rejected (jazz work as constellatory play of distinction in communion, and between black life and how it shows up in the mainstream)—we find a creative practice that bears little resemblance to the culture-industry drudge Adorno characterizes it as.[2] In fact, it may be that jazz work is also able to present a prototype for alternative forms of social organization. The possibility of this source of critical activity demands consideration.

In the absence of creative autonomy, how does jazz achieve its critical distance? How do expressive practices that are inextricably tied to—and, indeed, are dependent on—extra-artistic material develop with the independence necessary for effective opposition? How is it possible for heteronomous expressive work to stand apart from the general social field? Building on discussions concerning peculiarities of black subjectivity presented in Chapter 1, I will argue in this chapter that it is essential to consider black expression's attuned-outsiderness within the specific historical and material conditions from which it emerged. These conditions provide an alternative vantage point to that of radical music of the European tradition. The heart of the discussion will rest on a reading of Nahum Chandler's illuminating interpretation of W. E. B. Du Bois's set of ideas about the unsettling, yet potentially revelatory, sensation of "looking at one's self through the eyes of others." This analytic provides an invaluable framework through which to better appreciate the distinct conditions under which the black modern was (is) formed.[3] Within jazz studies, double consciousness is often taken to narrowly denote the "transculturation" and "creolization" that has helped shape the tradition. Here I will draw to the fore the significance of the contradictory nature of African America—the critical character of its obligatory retention of two conflicting positions: that of heterogeneous difference (inhuman, African, internally differentiated) and that of the hegemon (human, white, tending toward homogeneity and resolution). I am keen to show how the reduction of African captives to commodity, coupled with the imperative that these enslaved be subject to the juridical, civil, and symbolic laws of their captors, created an insoluble contradiction. Alongside their near-comprehensive dehumanization, it was necessary that these captives retained the potential to exercise will in order that they may fall under the laws that enforced their slave difference; it was necessary for the enslaved to possess the potential to contravene the governance maintaining their subordination. Black America's enduring embodiment of this illogicality—its impurity and its inherent, internal difference—calls into question the inclinations and priorities of the (supposedly) pure, transparent, unequivocal hegemon it is defined in opposition to. The black modern's predisposition "toward negation and critique" is formed and nurtured "by virtue of the very act of discrimination."[4]

The Social Situation of European Art Music

It is very difficult, after reading Adorno, to write on music without taking into consideration what this expressive form has to say about society. Music matters and is not to be taken lightly. It is never pure divertissement, even when it appears so, but is either a corroborator of monopolistic capitalism or a voice of dissent that immanently rallies against the socioeconomic order and ever-advancing rationalization of modern and contemporary living. Music does not merely reflect the social and political climate but, through its formal experiments, can bring to light societal failures and present alternatives. As Chapter 1 revealed, to argue a case for jazz as a critical form, within Adorno's understanding of radicalism, may seem perverse given his jazz critique. For Adorno jazz is the archetypal music of the culture industry, a prime example of the acute fetishization ruining the cultural landscape. The freedom promised by its syncopation and spontaneity, lauded by its early commentators as evidence of its progressiveness, was "less archaic-primitive self-expression than the music of slaves."[5] It is not only that jazz is unable to set itself apart and reflect on society but also that it is complicit in its own captivity and in the deepening ruptures that continue to alienate individuals. Jazz, as Adorno understands it, is antithetic to radicalism. It is fully compliant with the uses made of it, with its commodification and with the false ideologies of individuality and freedom that mask unyielding control. Radical, autonomous works, while also implicated in "administered society," refuse to present the damage as anything other than what it is. In contrast to the role that "light music"—a past manifestation of popular music—had as a foil or source of rejuvenation for art music, jazz helps entrench the separation between popular and art, through its complete service to the culture industry. Adorno writes in "On the Social Situation of Music":

> In earlier epochs, art music was able to regenerate its material from time to time and enlarge its sphere by recourse to vulgar music. This is seen in medieval

> polyphony, which drew upon folk songs for its *cantus firmi*, and also in Mozart, when he combined peep-show cosmology with opera seria and *Singspiel*. . . . Today the possibility of balance has vanished and attempts at amalgamation, such as those undertaken by diligent art composers at the time when jazz was the rage, remain unproductive. There is no longer any "folk" whose songs and games could be taken up and sublimated by art; *the opening up of markets and the bourgeois process of rationalization have subordinated all society to bourgeois categories*. This subordination extends to ideology as well. *The categories of contemporary vulgar music are in their entirety those of bourgeois rational society*, which—only in order that they remain subject to consumption—are kept within the limits of consciousness imposed by bourgeois society not only upon the suppressed classes, but upon itself as well.[6]

This is a remarkable passage on several counts. In it, we hear of the acute separation of art music from its popular forms, from which it had in the past drawn for inspiration. The musical expression (and so also the experiences) of the subordinate classes used to find its way into the mainstream through its incorporation into art music. Adorno denies the possibility of localized pockets of genuine community within which this revitalizing expression can be nurtured. The passage serves not only as a condensed sociohistory of the relations between art and popular forms—culminating in their severance—it also acts as a defense for the absence in his work of any serious *musicological* consideration of popular forms. We will return to the issue of Adorno's evasion of alternatives to European art music.

Adorno begins "On the Social Situation of Music" by pointing out that no music remains untouched by "the contradictions and flaws which cut through present-day society."[7] Music is fully implicated in these problems, which include acute alienation, permeating all corners of life. Music exists apart from, but its autonomy is sanctioned by—and is, indeed, a consequence of—hot-housed rationalization and the fragmentation of society into a number of specialized spheres of activity. The functional freedom of music needs to be considered alongside the ideology of art for art's sake, which imbues the separation with an aesthetic value. The intensity of rationalization that accompanied the industrial, economic, and intellectual revolutions of the late eighteenth and nineteenth centuries is a factor in this separation. Perhaps more important, this socioeconomic force employs art—or art's status as autonomous—as an outlet in which activity that is not easily aligned with the overwhelming tendencies toward scientific and utilitarian virtues is able to thrive (and thus not disrupt the order of the rest of society). Art has a crucial role to play as a sanctioned, cordoned-off site where people are able to fulfill those impulses that have been all but expelled from other areas of life. Art's irrationality—its unchallenged, self-referential irrationality—is not only separate from but also inextricably tied to rationalization. Where art does appear directly, it is as a commodity, with the market dictating its worth. All music is affected by alienation, although this is manifest in different ways, depending on the extent to which a musical form is willing to accommodate the workings of the culture industry. But Adorno also impresses on us that all roles in society are, to a certain extent, "determined by the [monopolistic] market."[8] Tracking the historical development of European art music away from its social function within the church and the aristocracy toward bourgeois art helps to root Adorno's thoughts on the "torn halves" of music.[9] It also provides a way for us to understand the contradiction of music being both *of* society and set *apart* from it. This seemingly irreconcilable position is what Adorno calls the "double character of art."[10] Alongside autonomous music's being implicated in or at least reflective of society, it is also relatively free of extramusical function.

The work of a musician such as Johann Sebastian Bach, who represents for Adorno the closing stages of heteronomous art music, "still retains some vestiges of a direct social function."[11] This is demonstrated in the musician's continued dependence on patron support, but it is also shown formally in the use of shared compositional structure and a compositional open-endedness, allowing for improvisatory performance. In this period the bourgeoisie, although still lacking in political power, begins to dominate both economically and intellectually. And by the end of the eighteenth century, the artist gains freedom from the church and the nobility and begins to produce work that is more in keeping with his own outlook and ideals and with those of his social class. As Andrew Hamilton explains, "Since it no longer fulfills a direct social function, Adorno holds, the autonomous artwork can create its own inner logic, which does not refer to anything external. In its consistency and total integration, form and content become identical; the work *is* its idea."[12] Form predominates in this new musical era and in its masked disinterestedness is able to, inadvertently, report on that of which it after all remains a part. The historical movement away from functionality is key to understanding art music's suitability for critique. Critical musical works both uncover the "barbarism of totalitarian administration" of society and represent what Lambert Zuidervaart calls a "utopian memory."[13] This insight offered by art—of the present inadequacies and also alternatives to these—is not gained through a direct address. It cannot be read from a work's content. (In fact, this critical acumen is possible precisely through artworks' *separation* from such discourse.) In autonomous music the fragmentation experienced by the modern human is found "sedimented" in musical forms of the tradition. As Adorno tells us, "Through its material, music must give clear form to the problems assigned it by this material [that of the musical tradition] which is itself never purely natural material, but rather a social and historical product; solutions offered by music in this process stand equal to theories." Art, although isolated from everyday life, holds a unique and necessary function *within* late capitalist society and, as such, can do no better than simply following the internal logic of its form, and in doing so it highlights the societal deficit. That is to say, composers, in their hermetic pursuit, by working through the musical material left to them by past generations of composers, will make work that, to a significant extent, reflects "the social antinomies which are also responsible for [their] own isolation."[14]

Behind the Veil

In *Philosophy of New Music* Adorno accounts for the progressive nature of Béla Bartók's folk-influenced work by suggesting that the forms adapted by the composer emerged from "south-east" European communities that had evaded (or, more likely, had been ignored by) the accelerated rationalization that accompanied the transformation of Western European and North American economies. He writes, "Truly extra-territorial music (the material of which, even though it is familiar, is organized in a totally different way from that in the Occident) has a power of alienation which places it in the company of the avant-garde and not that of nationalistic reaction."[15] The idea that Eastern European forms had managed to retain their integrity because of their distance from the hub of rationalization seems similar to the idea suggested by the veteran/doctor-patient of the Golden Day tavern/asylum in Ralph Ellison's *Invisible Man*. On a bus journey north, the protagonist bumps into the veteran he had met the previous day at the inn amid much cacophonic drama.[16] Explaining the cryptic sermon he had delivered that day, the veteran describes the opportunity that double consciousness holds for a black person. He tells the invisible man: "down here they've forgotten to take care of the books and that's your opportunity. You're hidden right out in the open—that is, you would be if you only realized it."[17] An above-underground, a space where forms are capable of surviving in their difference, "protected" by prejudice against black skin, is seen as an "opportunity." It is obscurity within which black distinction and heterogeneity can thrive, and alternative modes of expression and thought are explored with fidelity to the black modern. As Ed Pavlić puts it, the space "quarantined by segregation . . . [was] not *yet* 'disenchanted' by modern forces [of] rationalization" and so was able to facilitate distinct forms of thought and expression.[18] And as Adorno allowed for those Eastern European communities that had evaded the machinery of capitalism, we can argue that, to a certain extent, black life occurs under the radar of ever-increasing governance, "down [where] they've forgotten to take care of the books."[19]

As we will encounter in my extended discussion of W. E. B. Du Bois's grand concept of "double consciousness," the critical opportunity of this veil can only be adequately appreciated when reunited with its sibling parts: doubleness and double consciousness. For now, I would like to linger in "the shadow of the Veil."[20] Recall, once more, the vet's words, and the asymmetry of being both "hidden out in the open" and seeking refuge "down here." This "place," defying the laws of physics, is also a situation of having your being scripted out of books, a situation in which your opportunities come about from cooked books, where historical debt cannot be settled because the record has no account of you (and has created no account *for* you). This pair of simultaneous habitations tells us something concerning the dynamism of black subject formation. It is a double imposition of that persistent but unasked question, "How does it feel to be a problem?" and of fortified prior judgment—the inability and lack of will to see other than what one already expects, what has already been accounted for, that which is already included in the ledger—that veils what Du Bois gorgeously describes as "an undiscovered country, a land of new things, of change, of experiment, of wild hope and somber realization, of superlatives and italics—of wondrously blended poetry and prose."[21] The idea of the veil, or "veiling," as it appeared in "The Afro-American" of 1894/95, helped refine a line of inquiry concerned with America's response to the black presence and status. Nahum Chandler writes that Du Bois argued that the response took the form of avoidance, "a certain denegation, which is the act of 'veiling,' hiding or disguising, of the basic question."[22] The response, an evasion, facilitates an uninterrupted realm of differentiated sociality. Imposed invisibility cordons off the "experimental" generative realm, "an undiscovered country . . . of wild hope and somber realization," where practices are capable of developing in fidelity with a specific experience and different conditions of being. This insight, wholly absent in Adorno's dealings with the music, is, in fact, essential to gaining an understanding of jazz's distinctive relation to, and its place within, the "torn halves" of modern culture.

Black radical thought and practice is animated by acknowledgment of the critical acumen facilitated by the veil. In Bob Kaufman's poem "Battle Report," musicians are characterized as agents of a covert operation—"One thousand saxophones infiltrate the city / Each with a man inside"—who draw in unsuspecting "greedy ears," assaulting them with "noisy artfully contrived screams." Undercover action is also carried out in "O-Jazz-O War Memoir: Jazz, Don't Listen to It at Your Own Risk," although here, perhaps, the offensive is directed toward future or utopian reconcilement, not for the sake of black people but for a reorganization of the human/American as such.[23] Amiri Baraka interpreted Charlie Parker's artistry as an alternative to physical retribution. He tells us through Clay, the protagonist of his play *Dutchman*, "Bird would've played not a note of music if he just walked up to East Sixty-seventh Street and killed the first ten white people he saw." Clay also speaks on behalf of blues vocalist Bessie Smith, who, "before love, suffering, desire, anything you can explain, [is] saying, and very plainly, 'Kiss my black ass.'" And he adds, for those lacking the necessary "second-sight" that "if you don't know that, it's you that's doing the kissing."[24] On these accounts one could view Louis Armstrong's Samboesque performance in a new light. Was the congenial, handkerchief-waving musician really an assassin, drawing in the credulous before delivering signifying blows disguised as docility?[25] Kitted out in vaudeville camouflage, was he not contributing to the covert "down there," "out in the open" operations chronicled by Kaufman and Baraka? Lester Bowie speaks of Armstrong as a revolutionary, who, cloaked in the invisibility cast by the veil, blowing from way beyond its opaque side, infiltrated the mainstream without detection. He tells us, "The true revolutionary is one that's not apparent. I mean the revolutionary that's waving a gun out in the streets is never effective; the police just arrest him. But the police don't ever know about the guy that smiles and drops a little poison in their coffee. Well, Louis, in that sense, was that sort of revolutionary, a true revolutionary."[26] I am reluctant to detract from Bowie's musing, which dramatizes the supposed opportunity of the veil so well, but it is necessary to point out—by way of Du Bois's (and Ellison's) instruction—that whether gun-waving or poison-slipping, as it presented a problem for purity, black life had to be veiled; it had to be hidden when "out in the open" of the general social field.

Black resistance, much less dramatically, is constituted of inadvertent acts of nonabsorbance and nonmalleability, the problem of which is dealt with by the imposition of the veil.

At the risk of getting ahead of myself, I would like to say more here about how black activity in the general social field is often placed under conceptual governance. Aspects of black life that cannot be absorbed into whiteness are obscured, mutilated, or masked to help provide simple opposition to whiteness. It is behind this screen that differentiated, "chromatically saturated" black life occurs. "The Clown," a piece recorded by Mingus in 1957 on an album of the same name, includes a recitation over a circus-waltz motif, telling a story of black desire for recognition, but it helps to appreciate that what appears above-underground is often a denigration of complexity and depth. The clown has, according to Mingus, "all these wonderful things going on inside . . . all these greens and yellows, all these oranges."[27] Ellison tells of how mainstream literature presents the African American, "a most complex example of Western man . . . , [as] an oversimplified clown. . . . Seldom is he drawn as that sensitively focused process of opposites, of good and evil, of instinct and intellect, of passion and spirituality, which great literary art has projected as the image of man."[28] The clown's audience has no interest in the possible range of experience, represented by the clown's carefully planned routines, which show the breadth and depth of his creativity. They are, however, completely enthralled by an accidental slapstick moment. The lack of interest in his colorful repertoire—the greens, the yellows, the oranges—in favor of its melding into a murky gray, brings the clown widespread success and popularity. At the end of the piece, in desperation, the clown takes his own life, which is met with raucous laughter. The audience is unable to recognize his blackness/humanity even in this extreme act.

The Critical Potential of Being a Problem

Early in "Of Our Spiritual Strivings" W. E. B. Du Bois makes the following declaration:

> After the Egyptian and Indian, the Greek and Roman, the Teuton and Mongolian, the Negro is a sort of seventh son, born with a veil, and gifted with second-sight in this American world,—a world which yields him no true self-consciousness, but only lets him see himself through the revelation of the other world. It is a peculiar sensation, this double-consciousness, this sense of always

> looking at one's self through the eyes of others, of measuring one's soul by the tape of a world that looks on in amused contempt and pity. One ever feels his twoness,—an American, a Negro; two souls, two thoughts, two unreconciled strivings; two warring ideals in one dark body, whose dogged strength alone keeps it from being torn asunder.[29]

Without diminishing the importance of cultural hybridity, highlighted in readings by scholars such as Ingrid Monson and David Borgo, I would like to attempt a more far-reaching understanding of "double consciousness," toward an appreciation of how it might manifest in the music and, particularly, its role in the critical potential that black expression holds.[30] I have found Monson's engagement with the concept, and the passing but shrewd reference to Nahum Chandler's uncommon insight, an invaluable stimulus in formulating a response to Adorno's misunderstanding of jazz. As we will see, syncopation and swing, thought by Adorno to be evidence of culture industry affirmation, are in fact expressions of the double consciousness that structures black subjectivity and, important for the discussions that occupy this book, are sites of critical potential.

Creolization within jazz, referring to interplay or synthesis of disparate cultural heritages—and, specifically, to the heterogeneity of its musical sources—is accepted by all but the most Afrocentric of commentators. Amiri Baraka, who writes that "Afro-American art is an ideological reflection of Afro-American life and culture," also recognizes that "Afro-American use of African rhythm is . . . 'integrated' with European musical conventions."[31] There is broad acceptance, including among those committed to strictly Afrological narratives and analysis, that the tradition has, throughout its history, drawn from a myriad of influences.[32] In a characteristically dispassionate exploration of the centrality of African and European admixture in the establishment and development of the tradition, Monson cautions against unreflective accounts of synthesis that inadvertently obscure and minimize African American experience: "The denial of difference in a cultural field such as jazz, in which African Americans have always been dominant, has often resulted in a failure to acknowledge the influence of African American cultural sensibilities on American society more broadly."[33] The portrayal of early twentieth-century New Orleans as a city teeming with "brass bands, singing street vendors, black string quartets playing classical European dances (schottisches, mazurkas, quadrilles) and ragtime, and a whole variety of others . . . [along with] blues from the rag man," cannot be dismissed as romantic fantasy.[34] It is, perhaps, nostalgia, fueled by this "gumbo" narrative, that has led to cursory renderings of double consciousness that fuse it to a nebulous multiculturalism, defusing the specificity of the modern narrative that Du Bois was carefully reconstructing in his constellation of ideas. Consider the following interpretation from David Borgo, for whom double consciousness denotes a synthesis of disparate cultural sources: "Jazz music has exhibited, to loosely borrow W. E. B. Du Bois' well-known phrase, something of a double consciousness. Much of the impetus for past and present scholarship in jazz studies has been to gain a more nuanced understanding of the ways in which African and European values, resources and imperatives have combined and continue to recombine in this music. From the earliest meetings of downtown Creoles of Color and uptown Negroes in turn-of-the-century New Orleans, jazz has been a multi-cultural music."[35]

Borgo is not alone in using the term to refer to a marriage of European and African (American) musical sources. Monson, in gentle criticism of Afrologic perspectives, argues that the "vernacular gloss, which sets 'the black way' against 'the white way,' simplifies a long historical process of cultural confrontation that has resulted in a cultural landscape in which African American and non–African American worlds remain distinct but partially overlapping."[36] Emphasis is placed on dual heritage and the interplay of separate worlds, which at times coincide, overlap, or synthesize. This redress of the balance away from what Ronald Radano sees as a tendency of Afrocentric thought to "reduce the complexity of lived experience to a static and oversimplified phenomenology of blackness" neglects the crucial critical feature of Du Bois's work.[37]

Consider the quotation at the start of this section, from the opening essay of Du Bois's *The Souls of Black Folk*, which is perhaps the most quoted passage in African American critical thought.[38] Within it is contained, in condensed form, the scope of Du Bois's grand concept, which I, following a broad but by no means unanimous convention, name, somewhat imperfectly, "double consciousness." This group of historically determined concepts and concept metaphors assists our understanding of the distinct social, psychological, and ontological predicament of African America, as it works its way through the trauma of chattel slavery and wholesale disenfranchisement that was left in its wake. I have already spent time addressing the veil and the communal out-in-the-open underground behind it. We also are alerted to the *sensation*, or *sense*, of double consciousness that evokes affective implications of "unreconciled strivings"—the feelings triggered by looking at oneself through another's eyes. There is also the gift of second-sight, the potential of prophetic wakefulness and insight. My focus, as the chapter proceeds, will follow Monson's own, that is, twoness, and, more specifically, the cohabitation of hegemon and difference. Taking a contemplative pace, I will extend Monson's survey with a desire to open up jazz scholarship's consideration of double consciousness to the historical-ontological implications of Du Bois's formulation, and, ultimately, to explicate how such a reading of the black modern forces a revised response to Adorno's jazz critique.

The African American was born out of violent displacement, geographically and ontologically. This rupture that inaugurated the black modern was anything but the slow crawl of Hegelian spiritualization.[39] The difficulty of their being (human, or less than human) announced itself as they awaited being loaded onto ships. As Chandler writes, "Even on these shores (of Africa), the question of identity would not be so much a question of relation to origin, for that, perhaps, was not the relevant concept. Rather, the experience or sense of difference or differences that specified identity as the difference . . . would be decisive."[40] The "problem of the Negro" in America came into effect on the West African coast. In but one manifestation of this unsettling difference, Chandler reveals that it is not only, or even primarily, that the enslaved straddled two cultural worlds, two sets of symbolic significance, two sets of ethical/legal obligation; it is also that the very institution of slavery, and its laws and codes of conduct, was built on a contradiction in slave/captor civics: (a) African slaves were less than human; (b) but in order for slaves to be held accountable to the laws that supported this claim, legislators needed to acknowledge slaves' potential for contravening them (which is to say, it was necessary to recognize slaves as human). The refusal to behold the enslaved as fellow human beings rubbed uncomfortably against the requirement that these alleged inhuman beings be recognized as subjects capable of breaking the laws concerning their inhumanity, to which they were bound. As Chandler lays it out:

> The premise of the idea of slavery in America and thus of the American law of slavery is the denial of the humanity of the slave, where the essential mark or sign of the human is the capacity to be or become a subject, yet the slave can be made subordinate to the law only by recognizing his capacity to transgress it, his will, hence his subjectivity. Hence, the law of slavery "had to" recognize precisely that which has been understood in the dominant discourse of right in Europe and America since the sixteenth and seventeenth centuries as the basis for a recognition of humanity.[41]

The slave subject is unable to be reconciled—at once human and inhuman (and distinctly, American and African/black). The enslaved were branded as inhuman in order to contain their presence within the general social field, but the threat of black will (slave humanity) necessary to hold them accountable to that legal standard frustrated such efforts. This unwelcome irregularity upset the aspired-to purity of a closely guarded notion of the human and of America. Chandler's reading of Du Bois alerts us to the fact that this predicament of white purity is inextricably tied to the "problem of the Negro": "This difference produces a heterogeneity within the general social field of American life and history, a field that would be organized according to a racist logic of categorical distinction and be given over to a narrative of purity, of the self-repleteness and historical becoming of a white subject, a historical and social being supposedly arising of its own initiative, unmarked by any sign of difference. It would be understood to realize the purity of its own self-image in every form of historical and social activity."[42]

It is clear that any generalization of black doubleness cannot simply adapt and map the specificity of blackness onto a more general social context. Rather, double consciousness allows us to approach this other context and its particular dilemmas by way of its relation to blackness. Chandler calls for us to "generalize and therefore radicalize W. E. B Du Bois's formulation of the African American sense of identity . . . to American identities as such and to modern subjectivities in general."[43] This suggestion is startling on first read (and perhaps only because of it being so exceptional that concepts formulated by way of black life be used to address society at large). We are called on to consider modern being as such, and white subjecthood in particular, through Du Bois's conceptual lens. The aforementioned radicalism is not simply that double consciousness can be made to apply to nonblacks—a Bakhtinian "we are all constituted by multiple and competing voices," which, if anything, tends toward a suppression of the difference in which blackness was founded and obscures the tendency toward purity and resolution of whiteness. Rather, what is most radical about Chandler's challenge is that the generality requires that we revise, or at least unsettle—or, as Chandler says, "desediment"—white subjectivity in light of the "problem of the Negro." This formulation that we might apply to the modern as such comes about from the violence enacted in the name of "racial distinction," the result of a series of impossible ontological contortions on the part of the enslaved/black. The "grounds of historical and social existence and identification were placed in question" by the problematic of blackness—double consciousness shakes the infrastructure of white being.[44] A closer reading of Chandler does not so much contradict Monson's "generalization" of double consciousness as explain *why* its white application is also a radicalization of it. I will now turn back to Adorno and offer this more substantial rendering of the black modern to set up what would be an upsetting suggestion to his ears: that black expression is not affirmative but rather founded in unavoidable conflict and irresolution, "which places it in the company of the avant-garde."[45]

Syncopation

In the 1953 essay "The Perennial Fashion—Jazz," Adorno corrects his earlier denial concerning the roots of the music: "However little doubt there can be regarding the African elements in jazz, it is no less certain that everything unruly in it was from the very beginning integrated into a strict scheme."[46] What Adorno gives by way of recognition, he takes back in his dismissal of jazz and blackness, more broadly, as grounded in submission and, as such, perfect fodder for the culture industry and other mechanisms of control. And to those commentators of his earlier essay "On Jazz," keen to soften Adorno's blows by pointing to the fact that his criticism was not of the musical practice, the principles of structuration, and the material—commentators who want us to extrapolate Adorno's note that "jazz is not what it 'is' . . . ; it is what it is used for" (i.e., not "real jazz" but its industry appropriation)—he makes clear that "the abuse of jazz is not the external calamity in whose name the puristic defenders of 'real' unadulterated jazz furiously protest; such misuse originates in jazz itself." He goes on: "The Negro spirituals, antecedents of the blues, were slave songs and as such combined the lament of unfreedom with its oppressed confirmation."[47] The implication is that jazz, as progeny of sorrow songs (and the apparent arrested development of black subjectivity), shows a long-standing propensity toward obedience and affirmation. This is as reasoned as Adorno gets in his dealing with black modernity. His inability to see past the figure of the bourgeois is depressing. Where, perhaps, the characteristic irreverence of his brand of Hegelian Marxism would be most welcome, he is dogmatic, approaching the modern exclusively by way of the dominating consciousness of the era. But it must be noted that, through this blinkered outlook, which understands the black subject as irrevocably subordinate and harboring a tendency toward sadomasochism, Adorno's condemnation of syncopation—this centerpiece and structuring principle of jazz, and supposed evidence of the music's freedom and spontaneity—appears to hold some truth.

In his essay "Adorno on Jazz and Society," Joseph Lewandowski offers a thoughtful engagement with Adorno on the question of the affirmative nature of jazz and syncopation. Lewandowski acknowledges that the appropriated styles such as "sweet jazz," which dominated the airwaves, particularly at the time Adorno was writing "Über Jazz," could not account for all that the music was, despite Adorno's "undifferentiated account."[48] Nevertheless, Lewandowski argues, "Adorno's critique of jazz retains a certain validity precisely because 'real' jazz is about just playing, swinging as one feels, and feeling as one swings. 'Real' jazz is about affirming one's right to autonomous, individual expression—to affirm who one is—within a social collectivity."[49] Yet in light of the insight provided by Chandler's deep and expansive reading of Du Bois, we must reject this interpretation of the music, along with Adorno's inadequate address of the black modern. Rather than obedience and unreflective servitude on the part of slaves, and the subsumption of "unruly" "African elements" into a "strict scheme" of whiteness, we find that the very institution, and ground of modern subjectivity as such, was dependent on this black difference.[50] To recap my reading of Chandler's interventions, and to extend them slightly: Africans had to be inhuman to fulfill their role as slaves and foil to the (American/white) human; black being's irresolution and difference (internal and otherwise) helps define the limit of white/American subjectivity, characterized by a tendency toward homogeneity. Simultaneously, slaves' potential for willfulness (this mark of humanity) had to be acknowledged for them to be brought under white/American laws (civic, symbolic, or otherwise). Both of these positions had to be held at once, and this corruption was compounded by the invasion by African elements of what it meant to be human and modern. The African American does not flatten social antagonism or ontological contradiction but operates within, by what Hortense J. Spillers terms "ambivalence," by which "we might mean . . . abeyance of closure, or break in the passage of syntagmatic movement from one more or less stable property to another, as in the radical disjuncture between 'African' and 'American.' "[51]

By way of this more substantial and accurate understanding of the black modern, we can return to this issue of syncopation and swing so central to Adorno's jazz critique. First, we must take issue with Adorno's musicological interpretation of syncopation. In light of his scant address of black America we should not take at face value his description of an "ostensibly disruptive principle" that never really disturbs "the crude unity of the basic rhythm"; an "embellishment" of the "objective sound . . . which is unable to dominate"; a subjectivity that has no real autonomy but is incessantly "beaten down by . . . the beat."[52] This is not to say we must reject it. In fact, I would agree that, from a certain superficial outlook, syncopation *is* a "swinging around" a beat it cannot or refuses to overturn. We *do* encounter in the music a "centrifugal swing," or "rotary perception," all of which, despite their, at times, unwelding expansion, suggest spherical, bounded play, maintaining hierarchical relationships between the syncopated/variation and principal.[53] This characterization of syncopation as a fettered dance of rhythmic variations, always in deference to a quietly metronomic beat, hits precisely on Adorno's misgivings concerning claims of supposed freedom. The problem with Adorno's description is not its inaccuracy. If we confine ourselves to the surface impression of this rhythmic play, if we are content with Adorno's dismissal of syncopation as a superficial, secondary element of music making, and, most important, if we accept the reduction of black life to a footnote, failing to connect the rhythmic phenomena to a distinctive subject formation, Adorno's conclusions might have credence. If, however, we take seriously Chandler's augmenting response to Du Bois's call—concerning double consciousness, doubleness, the difference that Africa introduces—we start to appreciate swing feel as a musical manifestation of specific conditions of black modern being—as a suspension of the resolution between contradictory but twinned positions. Blackness is manifest in syncopation and swing as the play between regular beat and heterogeneity of variance. Let us keep in mind that the black presence "displace[s] the distinction" that tends toward keeping the white, the American, and the modern untainted by difference. It does not accomplish this by way of revolution. Rather it calls white purity into profound doubt. It complicates and disturbs racial logic and distinction. It questions the veracity of unadulteration. Black syncopation is not only impure owing to its African elements—consider how swing might be understood as the result of a ghosting imposition of an "outside" beat, say, a 6/8 over the regular 4/4 or, more radically, a Yoruba Elewe rhythmic complex over metronomic insistence[54]—but also, as explored here, owing to its "refus[al] to abide by the oppositional logic" of principal beat against a heterogeneous movement. In doing so, it ridicules the imposed polarization. It holds both regiment and "variants" in one hand, forcing out into the open the duplicity of unasked questions that maintain a "racist logic of categorical distinction."[55]

Adorno is entangled in a problem of purity of the beat—a problem of black offbeat. He is right to note that syncopation does nothing to overturn the underlying pulse. What he fails to realize is that jazz emerges from a subject constituted by the holding of contradictory positions. It is a subject that cannot collapse into its hegemon. Putting to one side the outside "African elements," the black modern was founded in a subjugating conundrum that required it to be internally compromised. Syncopation should not be seen as an opposing pole to the main beat but as a shaking of that beat, a loosening of the soil around its roots, preparing the ground for its displacement. The doubleness of swing, the holding both counted-out beat and the plethora of micro (and quantum) movements away from it, convulses the structure. It is a curiosity that Adorno reprimands syncopation for *not* overturning the maintained pulse. He also draws attention to the untruth of commentary that treats syncopation as an emblem of freedom within a social milieu structurally unable to sanction it. He seems to want to have his cake and eat it, too. In light of the discussion that has occupied this chapter, perhaps it is more useful for us to consider syncopation in relation to Adorno's adumbration of the "double-character of art." Earlier in the chapter, I touched upon a sociohistorical explication of art as both social fact and autonomous—a trajectory from patronage, social function, and communality toward hermetic independence. Adorno also identifies this double character within artistic production and aesthetics. He tells us in *Aesthetic Theory* that "art is true insofar as what speaks out of it—indeed, it itself—is conflicting and unreconciled. . . . Art must testify to the unreconciled and at the same time envision its reconciliation."[56] That is to say, one criterion for successful, authentic art is a refusal of closure; it is a keeping in play of distinction even as the work comes together or unfolds as a more or less unified piece. Speaking specifically of the conflict between the demands of an artwork's content and its appearance, but also what can be brought to bear on the numerous conflicts that occur in the production, performance, and appreciation of a work, Adorno writes, "Adequate performance requires the formulation of the work as a problem, the recognition of the irreconcilable demands, arising from the relation of the content [Gehalt] of the work to its appearance, that confront the performer."[57] Rather than dismissing syncopation as a pretense of independence under which "blind obeisance" prevails, might Adorno not read from it an "abeyance of closure," of conflict? Or hear an irreducible difference brought on by the imposition of irrational racial logic? Can we not say that jazz—and syncopation and swing more specifically—speaks the truth about the irreconciliation of modern life? Do they not shake the ground on which racial distinction is founded? Does not blackness and black expression as "movement of the productive elaboration of difference" contribute, in a critical capacity, to Adorno's thesis on the critical potential of art?

° ° °

In his book *Adorno in America* David Jenemann draws our attention to an obscure fragment from the theorist's engagement with jazz music. In response to Max Horkheimer's request for input on an early draft of *Syncopation*, a script by fellow émigré and filmmaker William Dieterle, Adorno's telegram offers this: "Scene in record shop ought to be high spot. . . . Suggest Kit playing six different records for different customers. . . . Six records should make satanic concert which by and by is integrated into one mighty jazz piece."[58] In these few words Adorno happens on the distinct condition of black subjectivity and character of jazz music. His insistence that this climactic scene be a "satanic concert," performed by an ensemble of six gramophones, echoes a persistent theme in black readings of the music, starting with Ellison's invisible man speaking of his desire "to hear five recordings of Louis Armstrong playing and singing 'What Did I Do to Be So Black and Blue?'—all at the same time."[59] In a recent talk at the New Museum Fred Moten shared a disembodied portion of sound artist Ben Hall's *Some Jokers (for Five Turntables, Basement, Ice Cream and Sloe Gin)*, a multimedia retelling of that mascon. Hall's syncopating turntables create a tremolo effect, a collective vibrato, tremor. Moten hears it as a "multi-stereophonic schmear . . . a caressive crash . . . black and blur."[60] This impurity of sound, this syncopation of versions, shakes our listening expectations and cognitive arrangement, sounding what we did not know we could hear. Adorno's thoughts on *Syncopation*, despite the vehement denial of jazz as a site of possible critique, inadvertently gesture toward the alternative engagement between black expression and radical art presented here.

CHAPTER 3

BLACK DWELLING, A REFUGE FOR THE HOMELESS

Toward the End of the World

Charles Mingus's bandstand tirades are well documented.[1] Met with audiences that were often inattentive to subtleties of the music, against whose "clanking glasses" and incessant chatter the "beautiful," "soft," and "silent" parts had no chance, Mingus took to smashing his bass, bullwhipping audience members, and orchestrating lengthy drum solos in protest.[2] He offered the suggestion that, money aside, the jazz musician would find greater satisfaction "playing in parks and simple places."[3] A street corner, or a friend of a friend's front room, maybe—venues not equipped to appropriate or monetize sociomusical relations; useless spots, in political, economic, and ideological terms. Squats, where the music could take root for a while, ingratiate itself to its listeners, become ingrained in the "household of the inhuman," where it could stay put, and where it could lead astray—take you away from home.[4] These are the places Mingus liked to play.

Mingus shows us—in fact, he embodies—the paradox of hypervisibility and mis- or nonrecognition. He exposes his audience as blind to black America and deaf to its music. The audience's ears are "clogged-up," keeping them from the "truths" that the music could tell—revelations, not only concerning black worldlessness but also exposing the contradictions that sustain the unfreedom of their own lives. On what was described as "one of those hellish, noise-filled nights," Mingus tells those who will listen:

> You haven't been told before that you're phonies. You're here because jazz has publicity, jazz is popular, the word jazz, and you like to associate yourself with

> this sort of thing. But it doesn't make you a connoisseur of the art because you follow it around. You're dilettantes of style. A blind man can go to an exhibition of Picasso and Kline and not even see their works. And comment behind dark glasses, Wow! They're the swingingest painters ever, crazy! Well, so can you. You've got your dark glasses and clogged-up ears.
>
> . . .
>
> And the pitiful thing is that there are a few that do want to listen. And some of the musicians . . . we want to hear each other, what we have to say tonight, because we've learned the language. Some of us know it too well. Some of us know it only mechanically. But by listening to others who play it spiritually, soulfully, we can learn to speak a little less technically. . . . [Jazz] is another language, so much more wide in range and vivid, and warm and full and expressive of thoughts you are seldom able to convey.[5]

The scolding is a rude intrusion into the somnambulance of consumer culture nightlife.[6] Mingus is challenging the audience to listen to, and speak of, the music in ways appropriate to it. He demands that the patrons see how ridiculous the situation is, comparing it to that of "an artist of rhetoric, with thinking faculties, performing for an audience devoid of concern for communication."[7] Mingus tells his audience of a gathering of musicians; he invites them to participate in the conversations that are being had and perhaps to learn to retell the stories they have heard. The reprimand turns out to be proselytization. This evangelistic strain in Mingus was by no means exceptional within the black-consciousness movements of the 1960s. Pianist and poet Cecil Taylor reports that he was "searching for a truth beyond the money principle—a truth that will make people treat each other like human beings." He continues: "America needs what the Negro has for survival." Likewise, saxophonist Archie Shepp shared the belief that "the Negro people . . . are the only hope of saving America, the political or the cultural America."[8] And, despite often being presented as a respite from this politically charged scene, John Coltrane's contribution, while not as strident, is crucial to this chorus proposing a universal black ethics.[9]

What I find most interesting about attempts to position Coltrane as apolitical and "universalist rather than . . . black nationalist" is that we are confronted with a regulative understanding of black political praxis and concern. This understanding refutes the idea that black protest is of relevance beyond its cordoned-off area of racial particularity.[10] Moreover, this is often accompanied by the implication that the music is held back because of its fidelity to black/African comportment, that it is redeemed (in part) by Eurocentric universalism, exemplified by Coltrane's music and conduct. In light of the discussions that have preoccupied this book, it is telling that Coltrane's embrace of the many and varied—his extreme "play" with musical material, his wish to play all the possibilities at once, his use of extramusical creative resources and commitment to sociomusical congregation—were considered contrary to African American concerns.[11] Coltrane was steadfast in his belief that black music could effect a change of consciousness within society at large, claiming as his community the "whole face of the globe"—"What we know we feel we'd like to convey to the listener. *We hope that this can be shared by all.*"[12] Black American "protest," which might, much of the time, be better understood as ethical intervention, is often characterized as exclusionary but, in fact, points toward a universal—albeit a black one.

Notwithstanding Mingus's frustration, it is fair to say that even through the "hellish" chatter of supper clubs, we hear the band. The commercial impositions of the club may make the music what it is not, but they also fail to access all that the music is. The audience will not listen "spiritually, soulfully"; it will not give itself over to what the ensemble wants to say, so the music slips away. Jazz is always poised to take leave of a situation in which its "language" cannot be heard or will not be listened to. The music retreats into ineffability, continually arriving at "a place named No-Such-Place."[13] The music is an intramural mobile squat—here, but elsewhere, too. Dwelling in mobility. It is always of "imminent departure" and "post-expectant" arrival.[14] The ensemble is "never done / saying goodbye / once begun." Mingus has what he desires, and he wants to share with us all.[15]

° ° °

In an extended dialogue about the possibility and particularities of black social life, Fred Moten, Jared Sexton, and Frank Wilderson offer a collective reflection of ground-shaking consequence. Social death—or as Moten prefers, political death—is the state into which the modern black is born: without protection by the law—in fact, in receipt of gratuitous violence from it; subjected to the sabotage of any sense of originary home (which in the context of open hostility means the denial of any sense of home at all); in receipt of incessant reminders of one's human worthlessness, on the one hand, and one's commodity value, on the other. Black life recedes from view behind this infrastructure of social or political refusal, inhabiting "a structural position of non-communicability in the face of all other positions."[16] Equality advocates tend to operate on the assumption that the antagonism between black life and antiblackness is a conflict between two unequal but mutually recognized players, comparable to the struggles against wage exploitation and gender and sexual discrimination. Minoritarian struggles are staged within the general social field, where, for each, there is a precarious path to (begrudgingly) extended liberties. According to Wilderson and Sexton, it is not only that there is no path to the comparable horizon for blackness but that the world is structurally dependent on there not being such a path and horizon. This is a fundamental difference between blackness and those (would-be) allies. At bottom, the problem of black life is not to do with social or economic disenfranchisement; it is not only due to unequal distribution of power and resource, but, more fundamentally, it is a consequence of a profound lack of relationality between itself and the world. As Wilderson tells it, "For the Black, freedom is an ontological, rather than experiential, question. There is no philosophically credible way to attach an experiential, a contingent, rider onto the notion of freedom when one considers the Black—such as freedom from gender or economic oppression, the kind of contingent riders rightfully placed on the non-Black when thinking freedom. Rather, the riders that one could place on Black freedom would be hyperbolic—though no less true—and ultimately untenable: freedom from the world, freedom from Humanity, freedom from everyone (including one's Black self)."[17]

In this book's introduction I touched on the idea that black folk cannot authentically appear in society at large. What we see of them is carnival mirror physiognomy—instantly recognizable, familiar and useful to the world, but disfigured beyond black self-recognition. Suffering and joy are disfigured in order to conform to sanctioned configurations—pornography and minstrelsy are but two centers of such engineering. The fact of black nonrelationality and, indeed, any possible extraterrestrial black life, is veiled by these mutilations. And in case I have not stated the point plainly enough, let me drive home the fact that—echoing Adorno's chastisement of jazz fans who "clamor for 'black jazz' as a sort of brand-name," who put purchase on "the skin of the black man . . . as much as a coloristic effect," much like they might "the silver of the saxophone"—the modeling of authorized, world-appropriate "human" life for black bodies is a profitable, forever-in-demand pursuit and one that tends to the safekeeping of the hegemon.[18] That which cannot be absorbed into ideologies of humanist aspiration and virtue can be used as (doctored) evidence to justify the interdiction on black life. Indeed, as far as this narrow conception of the human/world can see, these grotesque masks *are* black sociality. Sexton corrects this misunderstanding, writing, "Black life is not lived in the world that the world lives in, but it is lived underground, in outer space."[19] And this black beyond is unthinkable for the world.

The details of variance among Moten, Sexton, and Wilderson—concerning, for instance, the redemption offered or treachery committed by black expressive work; whether black death is social or political; and differences in theoretical genealogy—should not obscure their overwhelming accord.[20] All alert us to the fact that a world structured by the maxim "above all, don't be black" cannot but help sanction the violence against that life.[21] It is an inevitable consequence of a regulative drive that seeks to collapse black living into normative categories, conceptual straitjackets, as those living such lives look on, cognizant of this imaging but powerless to affect it. Crucially, for the argument being advanced in this chapter, there is agreement between Moten and Sexton, in an eschatologically utopian moment. Sexton offers, "The most radical negation of the anti-black world is the most radical affirmation of a blackened world," to which Moten assents, with matching vigor: "blackness bears or is the potential to end the world."[22] Moten's particular project, "49.99% critique and 50.01% celebration," involves what might be understood as outer-space exploration. It is a reconnaissance mission charting possible ways to approach the unthinkable—that is to say, ways to know blackness or simply ways to blackness. It is a performance of appropriate conduct toward blackness, demonstration of the disposition needed to bring about cessation of the "socioecological disaster" of modernity.[23] With long-time collaborator Stefano Harney, Moten tells us that resistance, a recurring "refusal of standing," can only be participated in "if you wish to insert yourself . . . into black worldlessness. Our homelessness. Our selflessness. *None of which are or can be ours.*"[24] They reveal blackness as a state that can be taken on by anyone willing to relinquish claims on the world.[25] Indeed, for Moten blackness is but one name for critical, disjunctive living: "This openness, this dissonance, this residual informality, this refusal to coalesce, this differential resistance to enclosure, this sounded animateriality, this breaking vessel and broken flesh is poetry, one of whose other names, but not just one name among others, is blackness."[26] In echoing Nahum Chandler's "generalizing" and "radicalizing" of Du Bois's double consciousness to modern subject formation, the black universality of Moten's ethics puts him in the company of Coltrane, Taylor, Baldwin, and Mingus. "Coltrane was a cosmic hobo," Moten tells us, "so even if I could be something other than a cosmic hobo, I think what I'm gonna do is embrace homelessness for the possibilities that it bears, hard as that is, hard as they are."[27]

Not Being at Home

In a 1965 lecture on moral philosophy Adorno tells his audience that contemporary "life is so deformed and distorted that no one is able to live the good life in it or fulfill his destiny as a human being."[28] What is more, we are subject to the almost irresistible pull to participate in that social life, to maintain our spot in this manmade ecology that, in contrast to that of planet Earth, is programmed to reduce difference to the lowest denominator possible shy of apocalypse. Our discreet complicity is required in order that deviance is kept in check without drawing attention to quietly fascistic tendencies of modern/humanist thought and actions. In preservation of our place in the world we fail to challenge the measured creep of ubiquitous, quotidian terror; we contribute to the ever-refreshed fiction of human virtue that masks an order that will mutilate, attenuate, and dissolve all that it deems deviant in us. Adorno's outlook is bleak. Despite his reprimand, he concedes that it is near impossible not to take part. We might try to resist by renouncing mass media—this is a recommended conciliatory course of action—yet our collusion is such that our thoughts, and even seemingly honorable intentions, are contaminated by the violence of modern technologies of control. On the one hand, it is impossible to live "rightly" in the "wrong life"; on the other, we are urged to refuse and to resist, in knowledge of the futility. To be clear: this resistance should not be understood as organized action. Adorno had clear reservations about such a response. He rejected direct political activism as an effective way to upend strongholds of "administered society," or to bring about a change in consciousness of the subjugated, clashing head-on with the student and workers' protests that were erupting throughout Germany in 1968.[29] Rather, as conveyed in his 1965 lecture, resistance, for which, he warns, potential successes are limited, must come from our reflection on the duplicity of the world. It calls for our utmost diligence in questioning the contradictions under which we live, particularly in uncovering that which an ever-perfecting program of rationalization has suppressed and rejected. Adorno proposes "a determinate negation of everything that has been seen through, and thus [enabling] the ability to focus upon the power of the resistance to all the things imposed on us, to everything that the world has made us, and intends to make of us, to a vastly greater degree." He contends that "little else remains to us, other than the power to reflect on these matters and oppose them from the outset, notwithstanding our consciousness of our impotence."[30] If there is anything resembling a call to action in Adorno, it is the exhortation to "not join in"—that is, to refuse participation in the upkeep of a fabricated world. It is to aspire to social arrest, to stop making world. Spurning cinema, jazz, and pulp fiction is not enough. We are to remain in a state of keen interrogation. We are to turn the most innocuous directive inside out in search of ulteriorities, to the extent we no longer feel comfortable in our own homes. "It is part of morality not to be at home in one's home." Indeed, we are to cultivate a desideratum for homelessness. The incessant bid to "join in"—personal banking and tightly packed after-school schedules are agents as culpable as cinema, news bulletins, and their punctuating commercial breaks—echoing through to the core strata of our lives must be countered by social adjournment that one should not pass in the comfort of home. To resist the torrent of social obligation, one must, borrowing from Fabian Freyenhagen, "arrange human actions and thoughts" accordingly.[31]

The ethics of reflective abstinence that Adorno suggests allows me to trace a path through Adorno's minimalist intervention to what we might call a black ethics, one to be "shared by all." To refuse to participate in a world that depends on our mistaken belief that we are stakeholders requires constant reflection on the language, images, and comportment we are asked to partake of and collude in. This reflection is not inoculated from society's dehumanizing tendencies; we tend to bring things, people, and their ways within our cognitive purview by dismembering them such that they fit our preconception. We tend to become ventriloquists, speaking ourselves through the alleged objects of our concern rather than letting these objects speak in their difference, and this trait, rather than merely symptomatic, is at the very root of modern immorality. Should abstinence also extend to the rationalizing tendencies of our thought? In our suspension of world-making, when we choose not to join in, could this provide opportunity for the deviant and routinely suppressed to speak forth? Rather than the arguably morally reprehensible desire to bring under knowledge that which is impenetrable to our advances (even when purposed with good intention), could we not cultivate virtues of reception? Or, to ask a more pertinent question, can we allow ourselves to be gifted, or perhaps messed-up, by blackness?[32] And would this necessarily involve giving up the world? A black clinch might take the comfort out of our homes. In allowing black life to enfold us, would we be forfeiting our spot in society? The requited hold might be a way to not join in, and this is, for Adorno, the necessary first step toward an unobtainable world in which "the thought of the many [is] no longer inimical."[33]

The relation between home and blackness is no straightforward matter; it is not merely an opposition of homeowner and homeless. Blackness, in its diffuse openness, is not strictly counter to the concept contained by this opposed duo. Indeed, as we will see, black life often plays between homeownership and homelessness, and—as we encountered in the last chapter with regard to subject formation—it forces us to reconsider what we understand by way of the allegedly opposed states. I plan to return to the broader and more fundamental encounter of blackness and home but for now will restrict my focus to this concept of home(lessness). The idea of home—whose constituents include, but are not limited to, ownership, the nuclear linear family (romance), and personal or familial sovereignty—is constructed to be unavailable (in any positive sense) to black folk. The structural denial is comprehensive, written into their being written out of the modern narrative. Part of this story, and a requirement of social life, is a desire for home—a possession (among many—and perhaps all—others) that, as a collective, the black modern cannot attain. Black people may be encouraged to partake in the fiction of a linear, nuclear private life, but it is seen to that structurally (through a matrix of policy, ideology, and economical and sociohistorical factors) as a group, they will not achieve this. A reclaimed, subprime, matrofocal, fractal compound or extended home is not a valid home. It is considered an aberration—reprobate repayment terms must be honored (after all, one should know not to live beyond one's means); patriarchy must be upheld to inoculate against familial and community retardation; one is permitted multiple homes as long as the nuclear hegemon is not undermined. "The pathologizing discourse within which blackness' insurgent *mater*iality has long been framed," writes Moten, "takes a couple of reactionary forms in relation and with reference to the subprime crisis."[34] The first attaches a ledger of criminality to the "black maternal" debtor, and the other, while apportioning some blame to unscrupulous mortgagees and to entrenched discriminatory practices of banks and realty, also reprimands the debtor as "a victim of her own impulses, which could be coded as her own desire to climb socially, into a neighborhood where she doesn't belong and is not wanted—the general neighborhood of home ownership, wherein the normative conception, embodiment, and enactment of wealth, personhood, and citizenship reside."[35] The discrepancy between homeowner and "victim of impulse" serves to reinforce the prefabrication of white moral, economic, and libertarian standards.

Ironically, this ideology of self-sovereignty lords it over the general populace as well. Adorno (in an admittedly surreptitious reinforcement of the bourgeois ideal) shines a light on the delusion of homeowner, under which the bankruptcy of modern life is screened, in his catalogue of modern homes not fit for habitation:

> Dwelling, in the proper sense, is now impossible. The traditional residences we grew up in have grown intolerable. . . . The functional modern habitations designed from a *tabula rasa*, are living-cases manufactured by experts for philistines, or factory sites that have strayed into the consumption sphere, devoid of all relation to the occupant: in them even the nostalgia for independent existence, defunct in any case, is sent packing. . . . Anyone seeking refuge in a genuine, but purchased, period-style house, embalms himself alive. The attempt to evade responsibility for one's residence by moving into a hotel or furnished rooms, makes the enforced conditions of emigration a wisely-chosen norm. The hardest hit, as everywhere, are those who have no choice. They live, if not in slums, in bungalows that by tomorrow may be leaf-huts, trailers, cars, camps, or the open air. The house is past. *The bombing of European cities, as well as the labour and concentration camps, merely proceed as executors, with what the immanent development of technology had long decided was to be the fate of houses.*[36]

This reveals to us that the obligation to "not be at home in one's home" must involve recognition of the false ideology channeled through notions of ownership and personal sovereignty. Much of our energy is devoted to establishing a position or state that has long been decided impossible to maintain. The inadequacy of modern dwelling is purely symptomatic of a homelessness already decreed by the "immanent development of technology" and the social engineering that is a crucial aspect of it. Adorno reserves special mention of "those who have no choice" where they reside, but his key point is that a fundamental distinction between those with the means and those without is, ultimately, indiscernible. While Adorno presents the private and individual (or nuclear) as embattled by malevolent social forces, we must, in light of the lessons learned from black study, also recognize that the notion of the bourgeois individual assists in the suppression of difference. We could say that personal sovereignty embodied in the possession of property—whether as a genuine permutation of modern subjectivity now past or as a persistent ideology—is a central player in an aggressively exclusive sociality.

To guide us back to blackness and where it rests (or moves) within this notion of home and ownership, I would like to linger on the first sentence of the long Adorno quotation above: "Dwelling, in the proper sense, is now impossible." We have already seen that a broad spectrum of habitation is deemed unsuitable. We have also been shown that, according to Adorno, a central function of home is the maintenance of one's autonomy (or of the ideology of one's autonomy) in defiance of encroaching social control and that in late capitalism such habitation cannot be found. And crucially, we are informed that this unavailability is only part of the problem, the more significant portion being that the modern human is incapable of being adequately housed. There can be no suitable home under the current regime. We cannot live in the homes that we live in. I am interested in this word *dwelling*, a word of conflicted etymology and a gift of translation that allows me to swerve away from Adorno's narrow intention but, perhaps, ultimately bring us closer to a central tenet of his ethics. A dwelling is a place we reside or stay. To dwell is also used to refer to when one spends some time thinking through an issue. To stay there and linger. To delay moving on. The word is a development of the Old English *dwęllan*, which sometimes meant to "tarry, linger, delay," but more often to "seduce, lead astray" (closely related to *dwolian*, Old English for wander). But it is thought that our present conventional use of the word, meaning to "abide, stay [or] reside," comes from an Old Norse source. The seeming contradiction between "stay put" and "seduce, lead astray" or "wander" is what interests me most, as it echoes a certain unsettledness chronicled in black expression and thought.[37] Consider, for instance, Moten's sketch of the subprime debtor

> as guerilla, establishing pockets of insurgent refuge and marronage, carrying revaluation and disruptively familial extensions into supposedly sanitized zones. Deployed by the imposition of severalty, demobilized from the general project, she infiltrates domesticity, restages race war's theater of operations under the anarchic principles of poor theater. In this, she extends and remodels the freedom movement's strategies of nonexclusion, where courts of law were turned into jurisgenerative battlefields, where public schools and public accommodations became black study halls, greyhounds-contra-hellhounds, where fugitive spirits, sometimes misconstrued as evil or void even by themselves, take freedom rides on occasions that parallel the radical commensality of the counter-lunch. The subprime debtor, in the black radical tradition of making a way out of no way (out), is also a freedom fighter, a community disorganizer, a suburban planner.[38]

Here, the subprime debtor is part of the resistance, playing with the way she is showing up in the world, much like Louis Armstrong's smiling assassin who slips poison into our coffee. You may think they are there, and that they want your home or your neighborhood—particularly when they sing, "I'm white, inside / But that don't help my case"—but they are not there, at least not as they appear to you.[39] What we see on the general social field is a carnival mirror hologram. Armstrong and the subprime debtor are already busy leading each other astray around neighborhoods elsewhere. But saying that, they cannot (or do not) cast off the effigy that was made of them—they never can say goodbye, or, perhaps more precisely, they are "never / done saying goodbye / once begun."[40] So they layer this place, that world, and, where they await to wander next, "put one / place atop another," limping all over this heterophonic chorus of dwelling.[41] In an interview Joseph Donahue asks fellow poet Nathaniel Mackey—whose works are a treasure trove of journal, souvenir, and memorabilia that make record of this hobo travel—whether we will recognize home when found. Mackey replies:

> I think we know it when we get there. I think we get there variously, and we don't get there once and for all. I've had repeated experiences of and senses of home, and one of the things these poems are registering is multiplicity. . . . It's a sense of arrival, but to have that sense of arrival you have to come from some place. You lose the sense of arrival when you sit still. It's the getting home that strikes so deeply for me, that sense of having gotten home. But there's also a sense that home gets up and leaves after you've gotten there that propels the agitation and unrest. . . . It's as if you get there and home gets up and leaves and you have to go chase it. It keeps moving on. That's the kind of agitation and wandering spirit that runs through the poems.[42]

The restless staying put and being led astray by home / away from home running through Mackey's poetry and scholarship is where/how blackness dwells.

Dwelling in/on Blackness

Listen to Ascension.[43] *Do you hear the comings and goings of a quantum squat, an oceanic caravan ("there and somewhere else no matter where" they are)?*[44] *What arrangement of thought and action does it take to journey with it? How does* Ascension *manage to slip outside the record? Is that the world's end? I want to avoid speaking technically, avoid the straitjacketing of ensemble into motivic chains and modal centers, and I do not want to pulverize it into emotive mush. I will fail, of course, but this acknowledgment allows me to fall short honestly. I do not worry about the music or blackness, corrupting them with my coarseness. My words cannot touch what it is they are. I am only admitted as the music's orphic lover.*[45] *I listen with affection—"If you can keep me / I want to stay here."*[46] Ascension *leads astray from behind. I'm up ahead. I "hear without / looking" back, and I love without reflection.*[47] *Walking across the ocean, "a train orbiting abject / Earth."*[48] *But now here, over from the other side, how do I resist possessing the music that has ridden me thus far? To honor the lawlessness, I forfeit understanding. I am content just to feel (with) them. To not subject the dwelling together to structural coldness. Coltrane self-cautioned on an outtake of "Giant Steps," "I don't want to tell no lies (on 'em)."*[49] *How can I rearrange to speak with them, and share this "feel in the music"? Cannot describe how it feels. Listen. Perhaps I could semi-sing, semi-speak my way, not quite knowing where I go. I don't want to tell lies.*

How does one make Adorno sit down and listen to what Coltrane has to say? It is not a conversation he would want to have. As I pointed out in previous chapters, Adorno paid next to no attention to how black people fared in the modern world, an outrageous omission considering how chattel slavery facilitated the growth and dominance of capitalism and how entangled the humanities were in providing extenuating reason for black subordination. His focus was squarely on what he considered the most advanced consciousness of the era, that of the bourgeoisie, with all other positions being addressed through this privileged group. Also, as discussed in preceding chapters, we should keep in mind that, although Adorno chose to write about jazz, and indeed considered its analysis as integral to understanding the contradictions that people were living through under capitalism, he had a simplistic and entirely unreflective grasp of how jazz work was carried out, and he refused to consider, in any useful detail, its musical material or the principles of structuration particular to it. Adorno assessed the music's potential for providing criticism by standards appropriate to the modern European tradition (although he failed to extend the same level of analytic care). Are we able to arrange Adorno's "actions and thoughts" so that he might be susceptible to blackness? Disposition his thoughts in order that he might be receptive at the expense of his prized critical reflection? It is important to grasp that Auschwitz was Adorno's moral compass. It was both a singular, unmitigated tragedy and an emblem of the disastrous effect of technologies of enlightenment and terror on the modern subject and human relations. As Freyenhagen points out, Adorno's ethics were driven by the need "ultimately to arrange human actions and thoughts so that Auschwitz will not repeat itself," which would mean "to change the current social world, since in it the objective conditions for Auschwitz to repeat itself continue to exist."[50] Freyenhagen characterizes Adorno's ethics as one of the "absolute moral minimum"—the very least we must do to avert a repeat of those atrocities. I would suggest that an ethics in response to black social death might be considered one of the absolute moral maximum. This would be the best that the human could do. To observe would be to take the moral capacity of the human to its absolute limit. It would take the human subject beyond the end of the world. Human and world would break up as they came into black atmosphere.

I am interested in engaging Adorno in a black ethics by way of his thoughts on music listening. As I have touched on at various points in this book, Adorno considered the spell under which humanity had fallen to be comprehensive, sparing no sphere of life (not even that of relatively autonomous expression) from the rationalizing tendencies that flatten kinks of distinction, recruiting us to participate in the ironing down of our own difference. For Adorno a defining characteristic of radicalism is defiance of dehumanization. Autonomous musical works—the manner in which they come together in synthesis but allow for particulars to stand in independence, their fidelity to the law of their form (unique to each authentic work), their commitment to working through the problems and opportunities passed down from an intergenerational gathering of composers—speak of ways of being that contradict the governing drive toward homogenization and separation.[51] Listening to music can also be understood as an activity to which moral judgment can be applied. It should be noted that Adorno took some care to avoid the appearance of outright elitism. In his *Introduction to the Sociology of Music* he himself—an upper-strata listener swamped by posturing elites (few of whom would qualify as "expert listeners" but often with near-adequate capacity owing to the relative freedoms of their class)—had enough self-awareness to realize that to behave "as if mankind existed for the sake of good listening would be . . . grotesque." But the alternative fantasy, that "music exists for mankind, merely puts a humane face on the furtherance of thought in exchange categories—a way of thinking to which everything that exists is only a means for something else."[52] The moral unpinning of his "Types of Musical Conduct" is clear: the way in which a type of music thinks, and so the language we must learn for it, is inextricably tied to underlying attitudes of societal resistance or affirmation.

Structural listening is the standard—to the point of invisibility—in academic musical analysis. The musical work is approached by way of its score as a hermetic text, overwhelming attention being paid to its harmonic and melodic constituents—this being particularly true of works of the classical and romantic periods. Musicologist Rose Subotnik writes, "Structural listening purports to account for every detail of a concrete musical logic, [but] it depreciates the value of sound with unusual explicitness." Subotnik notes that for Adorno, sound is "that layer of music which, through its use of such historically conditioned resources as technology and conventions, bears the imprint of social ideology and allows the social 'neutralization' of structural individuality. Thus the status Adorno accords this 'manifest' (as opposed to 'latent') layer is not privileged, to say the least."[53] The sounding object has become increasingly important in music scholarship, but the structural listener is focused on the score, which Adorno considered the closest one can get to a composition's logic—and logic here refers to more than composer intention and takes in the inadvertent play of constituents of sedimented musical material within the work.[54] It is an acutely rationalist approach that demands of the listener focused and critically engaged examination of the unfolding musical thought. For Adorno, structural listening allows those with the necessary training, and, moreover, those equipped with the capacity for critical reflection, to follow the composition in its unadulterated manifestation. Such listening is a highly rational affair, a mode of conduct, in which the structural listener demonstrates the "moral good" through her or his faithfulness to formalism. Moreover, the capacity to reflect critically, to take a critical stand—"the ability (and courage) to think and judge for oneself," to be autonomous—is considered a requisite for an ethics of refusal.[55]

It is no coincidence that reflection in autonomy is an indispensable feature of Adorno's structural listener. As Subotnik writes, "Adorno never sees himself as having to choose between structural and moral value, because for Adorno the two are essentially synonymous; 'no music has the slightest esthetic worth,' he asserts, 'if it is not socially true.' "[56] As atomistic listeners, we can be judged in terms of our inclination to push back against society by way of critical reflection on the music we listen to. Subotnik again: "the principle on which structural listening relies more than any other to authenticate value is not one of self-evident rationality but rather one of its own choosing: individuality. . . . Adorno emphasize[s] the responsibility of the conscious individual, whether composing or listening, to clarify actively the internal intelligibility of a structure, a process that, ideally, frees the meaning of that structure from social distortion and manipulation."[57] Despite Adorno's intention, this approach impedes the work's coming forth by way of its "own chosen premises." It in fact distances us from some types of musical practice and from certain aspects of all musical practices that do not fall under the radar of critical reflection. Moreover, and, as we will see, crucial to the argument unfolding in this chapter, structural listening "do[es] not encourage an open-ended sensitivity"—what I have been referring to as receptivity and susceptibility.[58]

Moments like these—attempting to reconcile Adorno's indispensable insight on the dehumanizing tendencies of Western civilization with this aggressively exclusionary approach to music—give me pause to consider the limits of his self-cognizance. It recalls other such indefensible moments but, more seriously, points to a fundamental flaw in a body of work committed to a reconcilement of humanity, scholarship driven by a desire to allow suffering, the nonidentical, and the unthought to speak. It is impossible to dismiss as an aberration an essay devoted to the supposed regressive character of jazz, which proceeds to silence the music in order that it fit a wholly inappropriate formalist agenda. One may experience a moment of optimism when Adorno tells us that "popular music commands its own listening habits," yet the lame attempt to understand those demands, and the deafness feigned or betrayed in lackluster analysis, is all the more infuriating for the positing of structural listening as the only possible means to the music itself.[59] "The notion of musical logic has been used by Western musicology for generations to justify excluding non-Western music from the mainstream of musical study." Subotnik was not responding directly to Adorno here, but there is no reason to doubt she had him in mind. She continues: "Western musical thought [has] a quality of restrictiveness—a quality that should not, however, be mistaken for rigor."[60] Internal musical logic is what guides Adorno's approach to "listening." Or rather, it is the individual, and the safeguarding of this ideal of the reflective individual, that calls for the internal logic of music. But what of music whose demands are not encased in the score, music that effects an erasure of the "original," or music that destroys the very notion of origin? What about music in which performance is writing? And of music that is impossible to conceive outside of the ensemble, whose principles of structuration encourage us listener-analysts to form our own groups from a plethora of performances that constitute ever-reforming constellations of intergenerational work? How do we get to the play with tone and grain? How do we get to know of the in-between tones and the warp and weave of timbre? And how should we listen to music that refuses to "coalesce," that has a "differential resistance to enclosure"?[61] How should we go about listening to music that springs from the "unsettled feeling" of "never being on the right side of the Atlantic"?[62]

These questions take us to Walter Benjamin's depiction of the storyteller, whose material is drawn from a "manifold" of passing and transient venues, "despite the primary role that storytelling plays in the household of humanity."[63] Storytellers are often mobile, not tied to home, although they continually return, and often to new ones (ingratiating themselves to their listeners), etching themselves into the collective memory of the human household / black dwelling.[64] Storytellers, like jazz musicians, meander and stray even as they stay put (a while). The close listening involved in storytelling, which may well be absent-minded, is not dispassionate appraisal of the faithfulness of the unfolding score. Listening to a story is not driven by individual reflection but rather by what Adorno might understand as "humility" and "affection." Listener and storyteller are in each other's company. A listener is open, putting expectations to one side—she allows herself to be gifted by the teller. This is a stark contrast to the novelistic experience of structural listening. "In this solitude of his, the reader of a novel seizes upon his material more jealously than anyone else. He is ready to make it completely his own, to devour it, as it were. Indeed, he destroys, he swallows up the material as the fire devours logs in the fireplace."[65] Structural listening fails to "encourage the open-ended sensitivity to diverse sorts of music that it promises," writes Subotnik.[66] Structural listening and the individual critical reflection that drives it are unable to orientate Adorno toward blackness and jazz, although addressing its shortcomings allows us to glance a promising alternative approach.

It is striking, yet unsurprising, that despite Adorno's reflexivity concerning its impossibility in the late modern era, the ideal of the individual, and individual sovereignty, in particular, continues to hold pride of place for him. As Subotnik reminds us, structural listening is less about the integrity of the work than about bolstering what is, by Adorno's account, a now-defunct subject formation, incompatible with late capitalist sociality. It is striking, but again not surprising, that critical reflection is the central requisite of the ideal listener. Critical reflection, or being compelled to "take a critical stand," is one of a trio of "virtues" James Gordon Finlayson has gleaned from Adorno's disparate writings on ethics—the other two being humility or modesty and affection.[67] These are attitudes, comportments, or ways we might "arrange [our] actions and thoughts" to approach what tends to shrink away from our advances or, rather, in order that the unthought and nonidentical might gift us with what we cannot help but suppress or ruin. Adorno tells his audience during the 1965 lecture on ethics, "if you were to press me to follow the example of the Ancients and make a list of the cardinal virtues, I would probably respond cryptically by saying that I could think of nothing except for modesty. Or to put it another way, we must have a conscience, but may not insist on our own conscience."[68] Modesty, or humility, or perhaps receptivity, susceptibility. It is interesting that Adorno tends to revert to "bourgeois coldness" with regard to music. Humility and affection appear to be of much less use to structural listening and the formal abstraction it yields. Yet, as suggested by my listening/dwelling with *Ascension*, if we are to take seriously the ineffability of blackness, and the blackness of jazz, we should be guided by such. We should experiment with ways to become susceptible to the music. We should arrange our thoughts and actions to allow ourselves to be gifted, or messed-up, by it.

On the 1933 recording of Wesley Wilson's "Gimme a Pigfoot (and a Bottle of Beer)," Bessie Smith revels in the "bad debt" of a Harlem congregation.[69] Spurred on, led astray by the antics of Hannah Brown, the "society of friends" shimmy and strut while eating and drinking on the cheap. They spend what they have. They give their time, their bodies, and their voices to one other. Hanging out together in the way uptown, they are not at home. They're so at home being out at the club, holding on to one another but not holding one another to anything. They are together in these "inappropriate" ways until the police wagon shows up. This is one of those places that, for some reason or another, fall under the radar of the control to which black life is most often subjected. Charles Mingus fantasized about playing these venues—a park, a street corner, someone's front room. Perhaps here his audience (and fellow musicians) would be able to listen in and "learn to speak a little less technically." I hear "Pigfoot" alongside another of Smith's, called "Nobody Knows You When You're Down and Out."[70] In this song she is a well-to-do reveler who, perhaps after too many nights in Hannah Brown's company, has lost all her money and the friends on whom she spent it. It is revealed that those drinks, good times, and the friendships extended were meant as a loan, to be paid back when the time arose. Realizing that the debt was never meant to be a good one—that it was always meant to be forgotten—Smith backslides into the hegemony of "world-making," insisting that if she got her "hands on a dollar again," she'd hold on to it so tight that the eagle on the bill would grin.[71] This pair of performances reminds me that while black people *have* to refuse the world, the rejection (their everyday living) is always up against the pull toward normativity—be that humanist aspirations of freedom and individuality or "the black" that helps define these. Resistance is inevitable but also fraught and fragile.

CHAPTER 4

STORYTELLING, SOUND, AND SILENCE

"The Storyteller," Layering, Heterophony

Hearing saxophonist Ornette Coleman play the opening theme of "Beauty Is a Rare Thing" as Billie Holiday delivers the bridge of "I'm a Fool to Want You" was an unexpected pleasure. This chance occurrence—which came about when I had two media applications open simultaneously on my computer—played out for me a fantasy quantum collaboration.[1] On the layered tracks I heard Coleman accompanying Holiday, weaving in and out of the sparsely phrased lyrics, playing alongside her, under and over her, then dropping out before returning to help complete phrases. Holiday sighs through the word *again* with an understated descending cascade backed not only by the string sections but also by drummer Ed Blackwell's irregular pulse (now wood-pecking roll) on the toms. The coarse legato that bassist Charlie Haden drags helps pull Holiday's own gravel into the quartet's frame, away from the overblown romance of Ray Ellis's orchestra. There is an undeniable kinship between Coleman and Holiday—a mutual concern with tone, tuning, and grain, and this use of the minuscule details of musical construction no doubt goes some way to account for the success of the "alliance." But there is more. In relation to the present study, the most interesting ideas that my chance listening experience suggested are to do with how music allows and encourages temporally distant musicians to "collaborate." Does it not seem that the tendency away from expectations that produce hermetic, self-contained works makes jazz particularly well suited to the kind of creative interaction suggested by the propinquity between

Holiday and Coleman? Do we need to accept the virtue that has been made of the supposed inner logic of the jazz solo? Are there not other important criteria for measuring the significance of jazz work/performance?

Holiday's voice—heavy, weathered by the years—was, arguably, at its most rich. Crackle and growl abound, as opposed to the needlepoint, bell-bright clarity she delivered with such ease in her early performances. This weightiness, the condensed grain of her voice, provided the raw material with which she formed her distinctive interpretation. Experimenting with the warp and weft of the voice's texture helped her negotiate the song in the absence of a broader arsenal of expressive devices. In relation to "You've Changed," from the same album, Fred Moten focuses on the "crack" of the vocalist's voice, which tells of a "willingness to fail"—the intrepidity shown when one is faced with the prospect of "partiality or incompleteness," or when we are unable to find our way back to an origin, or the Idea, which could not have existed anyway. He writes, "The crack is . . . [the] trace of some impossible initial version or inaugurative incident and effect of the resistance and excess of every intervening narrative and interpretation."[2] It may be that this "partialness"—the expectation to fall short, the embrace of failure—is what makes the inadvertent sounding together of Holiday and Coleman less peculiar than hearing, say, the vocalist against the incongruity of an orchestra. Could it be that jazz takes advantage of the inevitability of failure encoded in artistic pursuit? That it makes a virtue of irresolution and incompletion? Similar to how a vignette, told well, can evoke the whole world of its protagonist but retain an indeterminacy that allows for others to retread and rework that world, does jazz work have future reworkings of its standards and (musical and social) themes encoded in it? Perhaps a creative form that encourages a teller's or a musician's peculiarities—their limitations, even—will inevitably allow space in the same story for many others.

∘ ∘ ∘

A key insight from Walter Benjamin's "The Storyteller: Reflections on the Works of Nikolai Leskov" is what Andrew Benjamin has termed "iterative reworking." A story is a "plural event," each retelling both augmentative and constituted by it; the nature of the event is that "it will resist any possible complete self-presentation."[3] The story can never complete. As a "plural event," it has built into it resistance to notions of congealed monadic work-things. The retellings, the "working through," cannot satisfy all that the story is but rather keeps open the work as a temporally dispersed happening. New versions of the story repeat what has already been given but do so in a way that retains each teller's own perspectival and material quirks. Walter Benjamin refers to each retelling as a "transparent layer."[4] This transparency is crucial. It suggests that past efforts have not been covered over or surpassed by the new but have been retained and are, in fact, reawakened by and reworked in their play with the more recent and that these invigorating renditions are enabled by the versions their contributions help resuscitate. Storytelling, understood as a shared, reiterative undertaking (an endless, boundless rehearsal) involving a collective of disparate participants, both living and deceased, can bring to light endlessly evolving sites of expressive and cultural significance. I can imagine hearing the performances of "Body and Soul" I am most familiar with played all at once; I would speculate that the result would bear some resemblance to William Francis Allen's 1867 description of the work song chorus:

> There is no singing in parts, as we understand it, and yet no two appear to be singing the same thing—the leading singer starts the words of each verse, often improvising, and the others, who "base" him, as it is called, strike in with the refrain, or even join in the solo, when the words are familiar. When the "base" begins, the leader often stops, leaving the rest of his words to be guessed at, or it may be they are taken up by one of the other singers. And the "basers" themselves seem to follow their own whims, beginning when they please and leaving off when they please, striking an octave above or below . . . or hitting some other note that chords, so as to produce the effect of a marvellous complication and variety, and yet with the most perfect time, and rarely with any discord. And what makes it harder to unravel a thread of melody out of this strange network is that, like birds, they seem not infrequently to strike sounds that cannot be precisely represented by the gamut, and abound in slides from one note to another, and turns and cadences not in articulated notes.[5]

I can hear unmistakable voices—John Coltrane, Archie Shepp, Dexter Gordon, Billie Holiday, Betty Carter—weaving toward and away from each other, creating chords of varying degrees of dissonance and consonance, and alternately taking the lead as the chorus "bases"—here providing cushioned accompaniment for one another, there congregating (an ensemble of spatially and temporally dispersed "soloists") around the event that is the standard.[6]

There is a discrepancy between this sketch of intergenerational musical collaboration and what is considered storytelling in much music scholarship.[7] The word *story* is most often used as a metaphor to emphasize the internal coherence of a discrete cultural product with a beginning, middle, and end. The story unfolds logically. Happenings are often recalled consecutively or at least with an expectation that all the requisite parts "make sense" by the end of the telling. Its parts anticipate the completion of the piece; they assume that the story *can* be complete. Rather than an accumulative effort in which we see an amplification of the story with each new telling, as Benjamin posits, in jazz studies "the story" tends to start and end within a single solo. The success of a solo is seen as wrapped up in its internal logic, a hermetic pursuit modeled on the modern European tradition. The solo and the individual musician are the focal points in the jazz narrative. In this understanding, little or no consideration is given to the very particular practices associated with storytelling communities. Brian Harker hears a "folksy" ring to the phrase "tell a story." In his understanding, "less quantifiable elements . . . such as personality traits [of musicians] and cultural resonances" are subordinate to the internal melodic/harmonic logic of solos. The notion that storytelling in jazz is principally concerned with the "syntactic continuity and cumulative development" of individual solos is a popular one in jazz studies.[8]

Gunther Schuller, writing on the development of Lester Young's style, suggests that the blues is a paradigmatic "linear concept of playing and singing." We are told that "it has to be, and it always was. It had to be because it is a narrative form of expression. It is essentially a vocal tradition; it tells a story."[9] Similarly, Scott DeVeaux tells us that Coleman Hawkins's "way of 'telling a story' . . . was uncomplicated and emotionally direct." But DeVeaux continues in a somewhat contradictory vein, describing Hawkins's improvisation as "a continuous, carefully controlled crescendo of intensity on several fronts at once. . . . The relentless linear logic of harmonic improvisation served as the connecting thread."[10] Although it is not my intention to argue that there is no linearity in the blues, or in jazz for that matter, the suggestion that forms so dependent on repetition and cyclical movement can be considered as principally linear seems, at best, incomplete. The error of this misalignment is compounded by the attempt to explain the alleged linear character by pointing to the form's orality, when, in fact, that is an important reason to question it. The notion that a story is started and finished by a single soloist fails to account for the communal nature of oral traditions, of which storytelling must be considered a prime example. Much of what is written pertaining to the story-like qualities of jazz appears to be describing something closer to the solitary experience of the novel. Paul Wertico, in an interview with Paul Berliner, suggests something of this when he says, "The real great cats can write novels."[11] On these accounts one would believe that the story metaphor "simply mean[s] that a [solo] must have a logical structure, a beginning, middle, and conclusion, melodically and harmonically."[12] Yet treating stories in jazz as discrete entities with each solo being considered in isolation creates a tendency to ignore other significant dialogic and heterophonic relationships. Despite suggestions of autonomy and the preeminence of internal logic, along the lines often taken as given for assessing works of the modern European tradition, storytelling in jazz is also—and arguably primarily—of a communal nature.

Walter Benjamin speaks of the way a community—that communal listener whose attention sometimes spans centuries—is party to a slowly perfecting story of which new aspects are lit up with each further contribution. This framework of analysis bears a resemblance to, and indeed overlaps with, a wealth of texts concerned with repetition in black expression.[13] Benjamin's formulation is a life-cycle sketch of a story's telling. It also provides for an appreciation of a broader model of a slowly unfolding, never-to-be-completed, communal storytelling practice. "The Storyteller" sheds new light on the now commonplace concerns with repetition, versioning, and layering, and it offers a way to a clearer understanding of principles of structuration in storytelling—and, I argue, in jazz. These principles have to do with the creative tensions involved in retelling and "playing along" without forfeiting personal distinction (i.e., one's own voice). The story is at once "already there" and slowly revealed.[14] It is hard to imagine younger contributors free from the influence of their predecessors, so we should expect a certain degree of dialecticism. Yet the "slow piling one on top of the other of thin, transparent layers," points to a retention of a *multitude* of *renditions* and speaks of a parity between "versions" most often absent from teleological models of development.[15] The story presents a complex of repetitions, which can be seen as a sort of concertinaed heterophony. Extended, the lineage of versions resembles the notion of tradition with which we are most familiar—a chronology that sequentially links the earliest renditions to those of the more recent, often emphasizing development and areas of consistency. Ed Pavlić writes of black literature: "previous versions and voices sound in the present while aligning alternative versions of the 'past' in an accumulated repertoire."[16] The very same can be said of jazz.

When the versions are collapsed, one on top of the other, we hear something like the chorus described by William Francis Allen in the quotation above. We hear "the 'basers' [members of the chorus] . . . seem[ing] to follow their own whims, beginning when they please and leaving off when they please [helping to complete each other's ideas], striking an octave above or below . . . or hitting some other note that chords, so as to produce the effect of a marvelous complication and variety." This imagined "totality" of versions being sounded together, corresponding to one another but remaining distinct, would present us with a cacophonic complexity, one not only rich in discrete detail but one in which each retelling is cast in the refracting light of those with which it lies. This entails a markedly different idea of storytelling in jazz and of how individual performances (or layers of work) relate. Martin Williams's narrative of problem-solving jazz greats whose rhythmic innovations "surpass" and supplant those of their predecessors, and the linear coherence much-prized by Gunther Schuller are, to an extent, contained in the heterophonic model, but their linear approaches fail to reciprocate this.[17]

The story rests on the principles of repetition and incompletion. A storyteller will come to an end in his performance, but the nature of the form is that the story is kept alive by the expectation of future renditions that are encoded in it. Storytelling is a communal enterprise, and no one teller is able to satisfactorily present all. The collected experiential—and, in jazz's case, musical—fingerprints of collaborators age the story, giving it its patina. Stories are open-ended and are told in a manner that allows them to be repeated by other tellers. These prospective storytellers will inevitably light up novel vistas of the tale purely by the fact of the particularity of their experience and storytelling riggings—instrumental and technical limitations and advantages, for example. Moreover, we find that the open-endedness and incompletion of the story fosters an environment in which the various contributions can coexist. Indeterminacy and the active nurture of distinction are crucial to understanding the communal collaborations that emerge from these forms. The ruggedness of this layering of a multitude of individual grains is a feature rather than a bug. The particular ways identity is resisted, and the manner this resistance registers in the "plural event," adds to its distinctive character. It is not merely a story's orality—its being passed on from "mouth to mouth"—that is important but also the fact that it allows for, indeed demands, the individual expressive qualities of those mouths. The way the storyteller tells the story is not something added after the story has already been constructed.

His or her expression—the particular delivery of the story, its urgency or lethargy, whether the teller meanders in loquacious verbosity or shoots the story out in clipped bullet points—is absolutely integral to the words, phrases, and sentences used. Moreover, the playful tension within his or her retelling a communal work in his or her own voice and within his or her communicative capabilities is the prime site of creative activity. Benjamin's storyteller presents us with the model for expressive forms whose formative, or "unity-constitutive," moment is actually mimetic in nature.

The Benjaminian formulation of mimesis bears little resemblance to what we find in Plato's disparagement of arts—the second-order reproduction of the Idea or reality. Benjamin's twentieth-century renovation of Aristotle's retrieval of the arts (and mimesis) presents mimesis as best understood as an "inclination" or "attitude" rather than a resultant reproduction (whether copy or "original").[18] A mimetic approach requires an empathetic attitude, one in which the parties involved approach or adapt to each other in a manner that supports the retention of their particularities. Here a subject can show affinity with others, be fascinated by or curious about them, have them approach, without the fear of domination or subsumption. There is a yielding by both parties, but an empathetic or even intimate distance foregrounds their relations.[19] Expressive mimesis can show how mutual understanding can be made without the need to surrender our deviation. Encountering collaborative creation such as we see in storytelling and in jazz, we are shown "mimetic comportment" in action: a "sensuously receptive, expressive and communicative mode of behaviour between living beings who intimately adapt to each other."[20] It can be offered, then, that the challenge of artistic creation in jazz is to find the means to retell (often) established stories in one's deviance and with sensitivity to that of others. The work is in developing technique—a way of communicating (responding and playing along with)—that also improvises the various spaces of distinction necessary to articulate, sculpture, or find one's voice. The productive tension between the nurturing of personal distinction and the commitment to communal work is a creative catalyst and, in itself, a story to be told.

In jazz performance the distinctive characteristics of a musician play a prominent role in the making of a work. A musician's disposition, the assets and limitations of her or his physicality and experience (both musical and otherwise), guide the approach to the musical material. Personal quirks often provide unmistakable identification. Idiosyncrasy is a hallmark of jazz interpretation. Although the 1964 *Coltrane's Sound* performance of "Body and Soul" is a retelling of the standard, the gap bridged in this performance is not from the score nor from an original idea contained in the Johnny Green composition. "Body and Soul" the standard does not coincide with the composition of the same name. The former takes in the latter's melody and lyrics, but, most important, the standard refers to the plethora of contributions, from Louis Armstrong and his orchestra in 1930 through to Cassandra Wilson's 1991 rendition and beyond. "Body and Soul" is best appreciated as a site of "massive concentration" of significance that is amplified with each retelling.[21] In it is contained Chu Berry and Roy Eldridge's exploration of its emotive connotations (Berry's mournful opening shredded by Eldridge's double-time romp); Dexter Gordon's characteristic mining of associative meaning, taking in the lyrical themes of lost love and the body, as well as melodic fragments from "Giant Steps"; Billie Holiday's molding of the words *body* and *soul*; Eddie Jefferson's vocalese tribute to Coleman Hawkins; the 1969 Archie Shepp version that appears to play on the absurd sentimentality of the standard, slipping out of the overblown romance into a bop-laced sublimity; Betty Carter's almost inert "Body and Soul / Heart and Soul" medley; and many other contributions.[22]

There is an imperative in jazz to play a standard—that is, to tell a story—within one's own particularities, both physical and perspectival. A musician uses the tools at his or her disposal, often turning apparent limitations to advantage. Consider Charles Mingus's 1964 performance of Duke Ellington's "Sophisticated Lady" at Cornell University. In this duet the double bassist takes the melody while Jaki Byard accompanies him on piano.[23] Mingus was, by most accounts, a bass virtuoso, yet the timbre and register of the instrument make its role as a solo instrument particularly challenging. The double bass mumbles and groans, but it is also able to chuckle, twitter, and scream. Mingus, aided by his considerable abilities as a vocalist, tailor-makes an approach that plays to these qualities. Along with a display of dexterity across the range of the instrument, he utilizes vocal-like articulation—juxtaposing his bebop with blues-imbued speech.[24] Both the limitations and the tools that Mingus had nurtured shaped his contributions. Alongside the "'homemade' technique" that musicians develop, lived experience, both personal and communal, plays a central role.[25] This point may appear somewhat banal: we expect works to be reflective of their authors. Yet this experiential fingerprint is a central concern in creating jazz work. A modern European composer (and, indeed, performer) will imbue the piece with his or her character, even if the intention is to the contrary. For the jazz musician, however, the retention of this distinction is the focus of the creative process rather than a (tolerated or embraced) by-product. For composer-pianist Vijay Iyer this is perhaps the most interesting of all the stories we hear in jazz. He writes: "Musicians tell their stories, but not in the traditional linear narrative sense; an exploded narrative is conveyed through a holistic musical personality or attitude. . . . Kinesthetics, performativity, personal sound, temporality—all these traces of embodiment generate, reflect, and refract stories into innumerable splinters and shards. Each one of these fragments is 'saying something.' "[26] It could be argued that the most satisfying performances often display competence in "making the changes" and exhibit high levels of technical ability, but they will always allow the musician's own way of doing things to be brought to the fore.[27] As Benjamin writes of storytelling, "traces of the storyteller cling to the story the way the handprints of the potter cling to the clay vessel."[28]

Borrowing again from Benjamin, it can be argued that the standard is sunk "into the life of the storyteller, in order to bring it out of him again." This two-way movement is crucial, and in a sense, considering experience and the communicating of experience separately is misleading. Benjamin writes that "the more completely [the story is] integrated into [the listener's] own experience, the greater will be his inclination to repeat it to someone else someday, sooner or later." This integration needs to be understood not metaphorically but corporeally and pedagogically—the way to become a jazz player is to immerse yourself in it.[29] The storyteller and the jazz musician are listeners. Benjamin writes that "he listens to the tales in such a way that the gift of retelling them comes to him all by itself."[30] And this calls to mind the often-quoted anecdote concerning Charlie Parker's apprenticeship. The saxophonist apparently spent months listening and playing along with Lester Young 78s. He is reported to have "played them white" through repeated listens and would alter the speed of the turntable on which they were played, transforming Young's languid tenor into a tone resembling the effervescence of Parker's alto.[31] Similarly, pianist and educator Lennie Tristano would insist that his students be able to sing along with improvisations as the primary part of their training. Students tell of being encouraged to spend as much time as necessary listening to jazz recordings—not simply to learn the melody and harmony of a piece but to "get inside the head" of the musician and "live the solo."[32] Through sustained listening, the music becomes the musician's own.[33]

Sharing the Incommunicable

Walter Benjamin and Eddie "Son" House were both "blues people"—that is, those who inhabited "a period dominated by blues and its countless progeny."[34] Alan Lomax, channeling fellow chronicler Leadbelly, tells us:

> Although this has been called the age of anxiety, it might better be termed the century of the blues, after the modern song style that was born sometime around 1900 in the Mississippi Delta. The blues has always been a state of being as well as a way of singing. Leadbelly once told me, "When you lie down at night, turning from side to side, and you can't be satisfied no way you do, Old Man Blues got you." A hundred years ago only blacks in the Deep South were seized by the blues. Now the whole world begins to know them.[35]

The blues and associated genres are documents of modern trauma; conflict, alienation, disenfranchisement, and shock are all catalogued in its tradition. But shrouded in Delphic—or, perhaps more appropriately, Eshu-esque—indeterminacy, the blues is both more and less than these documents. The blues is a tightly packed corpus of story. It is a "plural event" (the tradition as a whole) constitutive of a plethora of "plural events" (e.g., individual blues standards). This story, passed from mouth to mouth, comprises layer upon transparent layer of idiosyncratic contributions—a sharing of experience by a communal subject founded in trauma. Does this swell of contribution suggest that incomprehensible experience can be recounted and shared? Despite the contagion—the garnering of immense contributions that tend to coexist parataxically rather than logically or dialectically—does not this very density, the overwhelming plurality of the event of a standard, suggest an opacity? Does this opacity give some clue to how the story can be shared without compounding the terror experienced? Perhaps to understand the blues can mean only to understand and contribute to its unintelligibility.

The backgrounds against which Benjamin and Son House present the "fragile human body" are markedly different—the various calibrations of technological assault in the one case, near-apocalypse triggered by dust storms and miscarried harvest in the other. But the degradation of experiential quality, and the schism between people (and the psychic breakdown of the individual) are common concerns. Son House tells of homelessness and the frustration of unfulfilled needs and desires that "drove [him] from door to door."[36]

The guitar accompaniment on "Dry Spell Blues" is a locomotive bounce that carries limited harmonic interest and near self-same repetition of the melodic theme. Even the rudimentary call-and-response blues convention is barely discernible. In fact, while the accompaniment gives the impression of movement, it is a drive that takes House nowhere—each door leads to "the killing floor." Benjamin, for his part, writes, "A generation that had gone to school on a horse-drawn streetcar now stood under the open sky in a countryside in which nothing remained unchanged but the clouds, in a field of force of destructive torrents and explosions, was the tiny, fragile human body."[37] Along with bearing witness to burgeoning monopolistic capitalism, and ascendance of evermore malevolent forms of mass media, this Great War cohort participated in a most ferocious degradation of humanity. Those who managed to survive were sent home mute. Against this background Benjamin accounts for a fall into speechlessness that began during the nineteenth century, as the spoken word of storytelling retreated into the novel form. The novel perfectly isolates author from reader, sidestepping the problems of communicability and compounding the silence. What I find most fascinating in this sounding together of Benjamin and House is that "The Storyteller," an elegy for a figure and a community once considered inalienable but now passing, was written as black song continued to be passed from mouth to mouth, a sharing of experiences that should have been incommunicable.

o o o

In *Aesthetic Theory* Adorno writes of the irresponsibility of artistic practice that attempted to defuse modern trauma by employing "cheerfulness." "The injustice committed by all cheerful art, especially by entertainment, is probably an injustice to the dead; to accumulated, speechless pain."[38] Adorno is not referring specifically to black forms, but his complaint finds a partial answer in Frederick Douglass's 1845 narrative: "I have often been utterly astonished, since I came to the north, to find persons who could speak of the singing, among slaves, as evidence of their contentment and happiness. It is impossible to conceive of a greater mistake. Slaves sing most when they are most unhappy. The songs of the slave represent the sorrows of his heart. . . . At least, such is my experience. I have often sung to drown my sorrow, but seldom to express my happiness."[39] This loosening of sentiment from its expected expression, whether by way of calculated obfuscation—an exercise of (limited) agency or bad faith, depending on which perspective one looks at it from—or of unintentional loss in translation, gives us a clue as to a possible reason black “storytelling” has thrived. Although this is a crude orientation, Douglass’s assertion that slaves “would sing the most pathetic sentiment in the most rapturous tone, and the most rapturous sentiment in the most pathetic tone” points us in a promising direction.[40] The prying away of a sentiment from the signifiers through which it is usually understood, the calling into question of the intention or feeling behind a particular vocal gesture, releases a pool of musical and lyrical material that is mobile, malleable, even seditious. This opening-up not only enriches relational components—gaining in prospective sound-word-semantic partnerships what is lost in dependable designation and logic—it also fosters an environment where contrary sentiments can share expressive material without loss of meaning.

Douglass again:

> They would make the dense old woods, for miles around, reverberate with their wild songs, revealing at once the highest joy and the deepest sadness. They would compose and sing as they went along consulting neither time nor tune. The thought that came up, came out—if not in the word, in the sound—and as frequently in the one as in the other. . . . They would sing, as a chorus, to words which to many would seem unmeaning jargon, but which, nevertheless, were full of meaning to themselves. . . .
>
> I did not, when a slave, understand the deep meaning of those rude and incoherent songs. I was myself within the circle. . . . They told a tale of woe which was then altogether beyond my feeble comprehension.[41]

Here composition is not instigated by formalized melodic, rhythmic, or lyrical design. Organic vocal utterance drove slave song, utterance that, at times, might, under cursory consideration, be dismissed as indecipherable “jargon.” Moreover—although this is beyond what Douglass presents—the separation between raw vocal sound and word or phrase, between verbal articulacy and “nonsensical,” is removed, allowing words to be heard as mere sound and mere sounds to gesture toward nodes of significance. Extralinguistic vocalizations—growls, sighs, cries, screams, and laughter—frustrate simple interpretation but, paradoxically, are able to pinpoint sentiment and intention (perhaps because in some cases they *are* sentiment and intention) with a degree of sensitivity that disembodied word and phrase can only hope to approach. A sigh might obscure a phrase to the point that we can no longer discern its phonemes; that same sigh may allow those petered-out words to be acutely precise.[42] When utilized in song performance these gestural vocals pull lyric away from linguistic comprehension, often to the benefit of a wider palette of communicability—our auditory capabilities bolstered by those of our haptic. The songs touch us; we feel (with) the vocalists we hear.[43] Robert Switzer writes of certain Africana song performance that, "Sound is 'turn[ed] against speech,' . . . until very often the words as such become impossible to understand (even for the intended audience)."[44] Contemporaries of bluesman Charlie Patton tell how his verse was almost indecipherable, that "he just brings that song out like there's somebody choking [him] to death."[45] This exacting utterance might be best appreciated not as an opposing force to designative speech but rather as an improvisation of sound, word, music, and meaning. What is being sketched here is a major constructive process in black expression. This dynamic dance is not a secondary tier of creation—the finishing ornamentation. Much of black song is structured by way of this broadened appreciation of articulation.[46] There is a play between blunt designation and indescribable precision. Raw sound may slip into word and music, becoming music and word to varying degrees. Chewed up words and corrupted musical phrases allow us to share what we are unable to state in plain language. We might say, in a slight departure from Switzer, that sound *becomes* speech and that such song-making continually redefines what it means to speak.

∘ ∘ ∘

Even when dealing directly with African American expression, Adorno tended to talk past African America, so it should come as no surprise that he fails to recognize (or, at least, to acknowledge) the irony of his embrace of a blackened art—one that becomes "voluntarily poor" to indict "the unnecessary poverty of society"[47]—in light of his sustained assault on an alleged formal poverty inherent in jazz. That said, his complaint against "cheerful art" (which is, typically for Adorno, underdefined but appears to refer to the material veneer—a work's surface—as much as it does the formal or constructive procedures to which Adorno most often gives priority) finds support by way of Saidiya Hartman's essential exploration of the disjunctive intimacy of terror and pleasure that characterized the institution of slavery—the "promiscuous coexistence of song and shackle."[48] Hartman shows how seemingly "innocent amusements were designed to promote gaiety by prudent means, ameliorate the harsh conditions of slavery, make the body more productive and tractable, and secure the submission of the enslaved by the successful harnessing of the body."[49] This administration of amusement was accompanied by a corresponding paternalistic concern for black contentment, perhaps driven by the desire for affirmation of righteous intention. In *Scenes of Subjection: Terror, Slavery, and Self-Making in Nineteenth-Century America*, the history of chattel slavery in the United States is shown to be the modern paradigm in demonstration of how terror can be "perpetrated under the rubric of pleasure, paternalism, and property."[50] Black enjoyment was (and is) inextricably tied to its subjugation, expressive practice being an important constituent of the governance under which black life falls. Yet Hartman presents a caveat with regard to this apparent, wholly involuntary, complicity.

From the account of his experience "within the circle," Douglass points several times to the incomprehensibility of the music to which he contributed. Those of the Great House Farm who overheard the "rude and incoherent" chorus moving toward them through the dense woods were party to sounds that followed little, or at least no recognizable, logic—linguistic, musical, or otherwise. It is likely that for them, as Douglass discovered was the case for their northern counterparts, the mere act of singing spoke of contentment, mirroring the institution's demand for black pleasure, or was otherwise received as "unmeaning jargon." In fact, the overlapping, competing, contradictory offering of the heterophonic chorus spurned even intramural identity and simple mutual recognition—Douglass himself admitting to an inability to grasp its depth of meaning. Drawing from this same passage, Hartman cautions that it is near impossible to state, "with any degree of certainty or assuredness, the politics of slave song and performance when dissolution and redress collude with one another and terror is yoked to enjoyment."[51] This questions the notion of performance as a realm of slave agency (and of consolation), but it also leaves open the possibility that black expression resists by withholding knowledge of itself. Hartman impresses on us that it is impossible to separate the complicit from the defiant in black song. The focus of her study keeps her skeptical of the critical potential of expressive activity so compromised by its participation in domination—again putting her in company with Adorno, who heard in black spirituals the legacy of slave songs, "the lament of unfreedom with its oppressed confirmation."[52] The impurity of performance—not only the weave of pleasure and pain but also that of complicity and resistance—appears to do little to frustrate the expropriation of black performance and enjoyment, whether the context be nineteenth-century antebellum, 1940s New York club scene, or contemporary hip-hop. On the surface any possible resistance appears as a mere pocket or thin strata of subterranean action, yet these modest indications of unseen depth open up the possibility of vast planes of unassailable expressive significance. Incomprehensibility, deep meaning, and incoherence are the markings of black radicalism.

Douglass's revelation that slaves "would sing the most pathetic sentiment in the most rapturous tone, and the most rapturous sentiment in the most pathetic tone" nips at Adorno's superficial judgment on "cheerful" art. I return, one last time, to the "Black as an Ideal" passage to deepen the conversation between it and Édouard Glissant's notion of the "opacity of black song," on my way back to some final remarks on Benjamin's concern with the incommunicability of experience.[53] Adorno's passage moves through a series of overlapping but distinct notions of how blackness or darkness is manifest, worked with, or aspired to in art. This is a variety of approaches to a blackened art rather than a checklist of requisite properties or actions, taking in a work's appearance, its thematic content, its creative materials, and its principles of structuration. I have already touched on darkness in radical art as a referent of an impoverishment of means or material. Adorno quite possibly had in mind the Arte Povera movement and artists such as Michelangelo Pistoletto and Mario Merz—the movement being contemporaneous with Adorno's writing of *Aesthetic Theory*. (I suggested above that the limited and rudimentary harmonic means of the blues—and we might include jazz—could be read as impoverished; indeed, Adorno does just this in his jazz critique.) In addition, rather than attempting to overcome the wretchedness, expression is charged to take on the *complexion* of the compromised world; that is, work may eschew the asceticism of Arte Povera but still carry on its surface the look of the degraded world. Adorno also highlights dissonance, again both as a principle of structuration (or creative ideal) and as the look or content of a work. He characterizes radical art as a "no-man's land" that shuns comprehensibility—work that refuses the disingenuity required to be understood.

To avoid being passed off as consolation, or as Hartman puts it in an interview with Frank Wilderson, to counter the "attempt to make the narrative of defeat into an opportunity for celebration," to counter "the desire to look at the ravages and the brutality of the last few centuries . . . [and] still find a way to feel good about ourselves," black expression must bear its blackness.[54] Its authenticity rests in its coolness toward appeals to enlightenment and resilience. Indeed, it allows itself to be swamped by opacity and, in so doing, contributes to its denseness. The layer upon transparent layer of contribution to "Body and Soul" or to "Dry Spell Blues," or the blues as such or the sigh or any other center of expressive significance, saturates such sites with chromatic dissonance, rough polyrhythmic complexes, and Babel glossolalia. These astronomically dense sites of black song seriously frustrate illumination from the outside. Opacity resists penetration of light. Opacity forestalls the communication of meaning. The communal, plural events of black work present what Fred Moten might call a "schmear" or "blur" of thick meaning. Their indecipherability holds us analysts at arm's length, and at the very same time they wrap themselves around those who approach without prejudice. These opaque sites—or what is darkened by density within these sites—cannot be grasped, manhandled, expropriated, or governed. Enlisting again the thoughts and experience of Frederick Douglass, concerning the misrecognition of black song as a sign of contentment, we can say, that which is "illuminated" in such works is often the image of white desire—the inquirer's face shone back from the reflective surface. Or to put it another way: what has been mined from black expressive arts, appropriated for general consumption (and I mean this to include the activities of critics, analysts, gig punters, record collectors, State Department officials, and slaveholders), is only what those miners know to search for. They, in general, find what they were looking for but, lacking the necessary knowledge, or, rather, refusing to relinquish prior understandings or the unremitting gospel of enlightenment, fail to appreciate the minerals particular to that no-man's-land.

The "opacity of black song" refers to a withholding, a refusal, or perhaps an impossibility, to disclose. In Benjamin's account of the storyteller's last breath, her passing rests on both a modern experience too horrific to communicate and the loss of necessary storytelling faculties. The black modern experience was inaugurated in horror within a "zone of non-communicability." As Hartman, with uncommon circumspection, informs us, we cannot hope to understand the monstrosity of slavery nor its afterlife because any witness borne is sunk into the blackness of the song. What comes to light is the labor undertaken by us spectator-analysts, so, at best, these stories must be considered compromised, interrupted by what we fail to relinquish in preparation for the encounter. The experience remains out of bounds to our thought, but, as Hartman, Moten, and others suggest, there is much to be explored concerning that incomprehensibility, about how such life, inaugurated in obscurity, comes into view in its invisibility, clothed in images and imaginings of a hostile society.

Appropriating Adorno's maxim for Samuel Beckett, of black song we could say: "Understanding it can mean only understanding its unintelligibility."[55] Indeed, the proliferation of black expression such as the blues is really the amplification of this (right to) opacity.

Empathetic Scholarship

The boundaries separating music and discourse are routinely trespassed in black expression. We have seen how the slide among oral gesture, music, word, and meaning presents us with musical forms that are most comfortable in vacillation. Yet within these forms creative and social significance can survive (and even thrive) and are usefully open-ended. Writing from a broadly modern-European perspective, the opportunity that music's equivocality allows scholars has been deftly presented by philosopher Andrew Bowie: "It is when we don't understand and have to leave behind our certainties that we can gain the greatest insights," he writes. "Given that this situation is in one sense almost constitutive for music, which we never understand in a definitive discursive manner, it is worth taking seriously the idea that such non-understanding might be philosophically very significant."[56] This observation is affirmed by Fred Moten, who in an interview with Charles Rowell argues that "even though music is not constrained by meaning, no one would ever say that music doesn't bear content or that music doesn't have something to say."[57] The relegation of designative necessity without giving up the right to "say something" may be the reason that some of the most perceptive writing on jazz has come from black literature: Nathaniel Mackey's serialized novel *From a Broken Bottle Traces of Perfume Still Emanate*, Toni Morrison's *Jazz*, Ralph Ellison's *Invisible Man*, Ishmael Reed's *Mumbo Jumbo*, Amiri Baraka's *AM/TRAK*, and Bob Kaufman's poem "War Memoir" are just the very first few works that come to mind. The freedom from semantic rigidity and adjudicatory commitments of academic commentary allows these ruminations to play on musical themes—"circumambulating" them, taking any number of attempts to answer, complement, "base," and extend. Moreover, writers are able to meet jazz partway. Their musicality puts them in an empathetic position from which to approach the music. In being "music-like," or being open to the manner in which the music tends to communicate, they are able to respond by means that elude most scholarly discourse.[58]

Attention is given to the molecular details. There is also an appreciation of the movement in expressive sound, meaning, and music.[59] Nathaniel Mackey's entire corpus is a testimony to such empathy, directed toward both the tradition and future contributors (musical and extramusical).[60] For instance, Mackey's commentary on Al Green's falsetto—mediated through N., the narrator of the *Bedouin Hornbook*—discusses the socioaesthetic significance of vocal quality and timbre, incidentally providing an incisive rebuttal to Adorno's comments in "The Perennial Fashion—Jazz" regarding Armstrong's castrati. N.'s correspondent describes Green's falsetto as "the dislocated African's pursuit of a meta-voice," and N. takes this up, writing that it "bears the weight of a gnostic, transformative desire to be done with the world." The search for the metavoice takes him to "an unworded realm."[61] We are told that Green's voice is "deliberately forced [and] deliberately 'false' . . . indict[ing] the more insidious falseness of the world as we know it."[62] If I were to pick up this call, I might further explore an observation made by Scott Saul concerning the incongruity of a corpulent, cantankerous double bassist and his high-pitched wailing: "Mingus takes to screaming like a very thin man. . . . It's more like a falsetto cry—a bellow stripped of its undertones but not its gravel, a man screaming unlike a man is supposed to scream."[63] Dean Blunt's work "X-TASY/Eddie Peake's Wet Dreem," involving an incrementally approaching siren accompanying slowed-down frames of D'Angelo—a mute but screaming angel of history—might be made to chorus Abbey Lincoln's encyclopedic takedown of the world in the "Protest" segment of "Triptych." I might then move on to consider how the wetness of Albert Ayler's warble causes havoc as it joins a chorusing of (often) vibratoless falsetto in pursuit of this metavoice.[64] This sketches an approach where the focus is not on individual solos, or performances or musicians, but has in sight from the start a network of associations that often takes minutiae, and what are usually regarded as secondary musical components, as points of departure. The extramusical and musical material that occupy more conventional analyses mingle and, indeed, slide into one another. The challenge for the analyst attracted to the possibilities of this approach is in learning to listen and in finding ways to circumvent the tendency to apply extramural and reified categories and expectations. One would need to immerse oneself in the depth and breadth of the tradition in order to become attuned to how these contributions gather and hang.

The idea that we should look to jazz practice to find more appropriate means to study and write about it finds an early champion in Norman Weinstein. Reminiscent of Benjamin's ease with drawing from the seemingly divergent sources of secularized theology, mysticism, romantic aesthetics, and

Marxist theory and praxis, Weinstein, in a short essay published in 1997, mines West African polytheism, African American aesthetics, and cultural criticism in his appreciation and critical adaptation of the Art Ensemble of Chicago. Rather than attempting to pry the music open from the outside, he uses an integrative approach that advances toward its object from multiple angles and registers, working to understand and contribute to it on its own terms. At the start of the essay, Weinstein writes that his intended method is "to tell it in the spirit of their music: in fits and starts, discontinuously, shards of themes as the tapes keep rolling."[65] True to this directive, we follow Weinstein's exploration from a discussion concerning the authenticity of wearing African kente cloth onstage to a depiction of the band's critical reappraisal of the minstrel favorite "Oh! Susanna," on through to a segment on the responsibilities of the audience-collaborator/audience-consumer and the appropriateness of committed political acts within aesthetic and entertainment settings, recurring themes around Yoruba pantheon, and a consideration of the opportunities and limitations of the metaphor as a principal tool of artistic creation and analysis.

The job of the critic is to understand the music, yet, as Robert Walser points out, "overall, academics . . . seem increasingly drawn to 'classicizing' strategies for legitimating jazz." In an attempt to understand the tendency, he continues: "Now, it seems natural enough that people who are trying to win more respect for the music they love should do so by making comparisons with the most prestigious music around, classical music. But the price of classicism is always loss of specificity, just as it has been the price of the canonic coherence of European concert music (the disparate sounds of many centuries, many peoples, many functions, many meanings all homogenized and made interchangeably 'great')."[66]

Answering John Tynan's infamous indictment of a 1961 performance as "anti-jazz," Coltrane (in the company of fellow band member Eric Dolphy) responded: "The best thing a critic can do is to thoroughly understand what he is writing about and then jump in. That's all he can do. I have even seen favorable criticism which revealed a lack of profound analysis, causing it to be little more than superficial. Understanding is what is needed. That is all you can do. Get all the understanding for what you're speaking of that you can get. That way you have done your best."[67] Fred Moten refers to his approach to the study of black music as one of preparation, a preparation for communion: "In *In the Break* I refer to Eric Dolphy talking about preparing himself to play with Cecil Taylor: I'm trying to write in preparation, as well; maybe not to play with Cecil but to abide with his work better or more fully, to listen more carefully and creatively and critically. For me, this sense of writing as preparation or even anticipation constitutes something on the order of a mode of inquiry."[68] As we have seen, this listening, this preparing to speak, is essential to being able to share stories and experiences. Clearly, this is an approach that can be attempted only by those who have embarked on the mandatory listening experience in which all jazz contributors are required to apprentice. As Andrew Bowie reminds us, an approach that wishes to avoid "merely confirming the philosophical and methodological presuppositions that one adheres to before engaging with music" needs to pay heed "to the importance of learning really to listen and play."[69] The experience of that listening preparation will, perhaps, equip us with the ability to speak with Billie Holiday concerning the opportunities that the encoded "partiality and incompleteness" performance in black song involves. Through listening to her, it may be that we are able to make the crack of her voice our own, allowing for academic work that moves toward susceptibility and a willingness to fail.

POSTSCRIPT

Some Thoughts on the Inadequacy and Indispensability of Jazz Records

1

The history of jazz is inextricably tied to the history of the jazz record.[1] We know of the foundational importance of figures such as trumpeter Buddy Bolden, but because of the absence of recordings, we can only speculate on the particulars of his influence.[2] To talk about the history of jazz is really to talk about the history of the jazz record. This point is hammered home by the fact that Bolden was a contemporary of fellow cornetist King Oliver and of a young Sidney Bechet (clarinet).[3] We have extensive audio archives for both. The lack of such for Bolden places him in a distinct historical position. The unrecorded tradition is the antehistory of jazz, traces of which no doubt still inform the material being used today, despite our inability to identify them with any certainty.[4] Through them the music can be freeze-framed for analytic and pedagogical purposes. Analysts—whether Schenkerian or Afrological, structural or interpretive—can discuss with some confidence the formal principles of the music contained in the format and the development, trends, and innovations that have shaped the tradition. While what is written about jazz musicians and the scene is shrouded in myth and half-truth, the jazz record gives what is most often considered the indisputable document of the tradition.

2

Jazz and the gramophone are often presented as paradigms of twentieth-century culture, two emblems of the tectonic cultural shift from old Europe to the United States. In distinct and related ways jazz and the record provide the background to the American century. It is not only that the two, recording technology and jazz, developed concurrently but also that jazz, as we know it, is utterly dependent on that technology for its development. While it may be a stretch to suggest that jazz would not have developed at all without records, it is surely indisputable that it would have taken on a markedly different, and less rich, character. I am trying to imagine Charlie Parker relieved of his Lester Young 78s, or Mingus's experiments on the border between composition and improvisation with the Jazz Workshop without him having studied Ellington's own trials, or what contemporary piano trios might sound like without that handful of albums recorded by the 1959–62 Bill Evans group. Abstracting isolated examples to demonstrate the importance of records to the tradition is peculiar for a music so intimately identified with this technology.

3

Oral traditions in music are usually transmitted from mouth to mouth. They rely on a flesh-and-blood teacher passing on his or her interpretation of the musical material to a flesh-and-blood student. Unlike the modern European tradition, within which scores allow for a certain amount of student independence, music that is taught and learned without recourse to texts gives the teacher (and his or her particular view on the material—its limitations and possibilities) much authority. A genuine innovation of jazz, and the record technology with which it grew up, is the democratization of African (American) oral tradition. Demonstration is heard on record alongside (and in some cases rather than from) an in-person teacher. Through recordings, musicians are free from a reliance on a telephone game in which they are only able to receive information several hands old. The antiphonic principle of oral pedagogy is updated and deepened as musicians listen and respond not only to their near contemporaries but also to work that would have traditionally been out of their earshot. This is key and absolutely distinctive of jazz—an oral tradition for the twentieth century. The further away we get from Louis Armstrong's Hot Five recordings, the more this fact proves itself. In fact, it might be argued that only with distance are we able to fully appreciate its significance. The pianist Jason Moran is able to reach back across generations of musicians to deal directly with Fats Waller. This is not to say he pays no heed to what occurred in between, only that he need not rely on secondhand accounts. He can go straight to Waller.

4

Jazz records are undeniably indispensable, but as a document of the creative processes of jazz, they are also inadequate. There are the practical constraints the recording process places on studio performance to consider—even where executives are respectful of the musicians' intentions or, more importantly, the music's particular work ethic, it is necessary to contain pieces within a listening format.[5] The studio environment does not even attempt to replicate that of live performance, and the efficiency demanded of musicians sets it apart from the rehearsal and practice rooms with which it shares some similarities.[6] All but the most commercially or critically acclaimed are bound to anxiety-inducing agreements to deliver the goods, so to speak, within the time allocated. Investors' returns are to be maximized, arts council funding justified, and budgets adhered to.

But perhaps most significant is the very intention of making a product—transforming jazz work into an object. This music is defined to a large degree by its sociomusical interaction—its performance—so perhaps the hardest thing to reconcile concerning recorded jazz is the congealing of the processual, the freeze-framing of work, the attempt to "complete." Of course, in a single performance of "Body and Soul" there is a beginning and an end. This seems to frame the performance as a work. But the nature of live improvised jazz is that we do not at any time hold the whole in our sight: we encounter jazz work piecemeal. This is the nature of all performance, but it is most significant to works in which the sounding object is made and lost from one moment to the next. In live jazz the idea of a hermetic, closed off, completed whole is not always/necessarily useful. At the end of a jazz piece one is often left with the impression that it actually continues in some other dimension or that it could be picked up again where it was left, that the piece has not—or cannot—end. The clichéd jazz ending caricatures this—its last chord or note a comma: where to next?

The impermanence of live performance, particularly that which is heavily improvised—the partiality, the imperfection and incompletion, the idea of a work in progress, the making and losing in the moment—sits very comfortably with, in fact, validates the lack of, autonomous internal logic that is held at such a premium in modern European music. And in fact, pieces are picked up, and contributions are picked through, again and again. The listener is party to musicians working on and through pieces made up of layer upon layer of prior contributions. Much jazz is like watching chefs who work in an open kitchen and whose menu cannot be advertised, as they do not know what it is that they are cooking. Jazz records strain between this open experimentation and an allegiance to the Western tradition in their having us believe that they are, in fact, the fully cooked meal served up on a plate. In the very intention of making a record we find an opposition to the structuring principles of jazz. The paradox inherent in the jazz record is that while the deferral that structures the music is obscured by containment within a product, this deferral, which allows jazz works to be augmented and kept open across generations of musicians, is wholly dependent on jazz being documented.

5

Walter Benjamin writes that "the technique of reproduction detaches the reproduced object from the domain of tradition."[7] At first glance, this does not seem to be true for jazz, but, in fact, this is exactly the problem with recording. We are told of and must accept the importance of the audio record of musicians to the preservation and continuation of the jazz tradition. It is hard to argue with this fact. Listening to recordings is the first and primary activity in jazz musicians' self-pedagogy. Records hold an irreconcilable contradiction in that they help sustain a tradition they are unable to reproduce in their medium, a tradition defined by incompletion, open-endedness, expansive or suspended notions of time, uncertainty. But while, for Benjamin, the exchange is originality for plurality, in jazz studio recordings, no original exists (or perhaps I should say: the original that does exist—the master copy of the jazz product—is, arguably, not what jazz is). Jazz work is not what is reproduced in records. Studio recordings, to varying degrees, fabricate the jazz work of performance, plays, rehearsals, and practice.[8] The prosperity that comes with them robs the music of a certain readiness to own "failure." The prospect of repeated listenings, both during the production process and after release, unseats the priority of a "willingness to fail" as musicians move toward the desire for documents that will stand up to close, repeated, structural scrutiny. In the recording studio jazz capitulates to the demands of a hermetic work-thing product. Although this is not what he had in mind, this is how we might best understand Adorno's infamous indictment, "jazz is not what it is, it's what it is used for," even as, ironically, the use of jazz, its abstraction into work-thing, brings it closer to Adorno's ideal of the internal logic of the score.[9]

Returning to Benjamin, the problem we encounter in the mechanical reproduction of jazz is not the robbing of originality by a multitude of copies that can travel across space and time but the fact that no original can be captured. And in fact this is not the intention of the studio jazz record. The studio performance is not just a poor substitute for a live performance. Although it can sound quite like the real thing, its very existence—as a cultural artifact, as a commodity, as something made complete, made before us and for us—appears to oppose the structuring principles of jazz.

6

Charles Mingus first recorded "Fables of Faubus" in 1959 on the Columbia release *Mingus Ah Um*. The extended-form piece, which even in this, its most restrained rendering, was over eight minutes long, was, on this occasion, recorded without the lyrics that Mingus penned—a satirical response to the deployment by Orval Eugene Faubus (governor of Arkansas from 1955 to 1967) of the National Guard to prevent the admission of African Americans into Little Rock Central High School.[10] Comparing this earlier version with another, recorded two years later for *Charles Mingus Presents Charles Mingus* (on the Candid label), Salim Washington notes, "The Columbia version sounds tame and controlled . . . whereas the music of the Candid version contains the same bravado and daring that are found in the 1959 lyrics."[11] On the *Mingus Ah Um* version I hear the cleanly enunciated themes of the A-sections as faux-minstrelsy. The romantic dreamscape of the middle section, rudely interrupted by the moaning whine, turns out to be a scam, too. It is, perhaps, not quite the docile performance suggested by Washington, but difference between the two versions does point to something pertinent to these back-and-forth thoughts of mine.

The *Mingus Ah Um* version of "Fables of Faubus"—and indeed the album as a whole—presents a polished, contained, perfected package of fetishized jazz work. It is not a snapshot of the creative process (as some jazz recordings are) but rather a completed, perfected sound-object. I hear it from behind the glass, as it were, through headphones as if I were not of its congregation. Raspberry blowing horns offer a comical, vaudevillian effect, but each horn gives up its distinction in service to the written line and synthesized sound. On *Charles Mingus Presents Charles Mingus* the horns are stepping on each other's toes; they talk over each other. On *Mingus Ah Um* they speak as one voice. No prodding or probing. No searching. It is made to sound easy. There is little of the goading by the rhythm section we hear on later versions, none of the Mingus/Richmond harrying. Solos are lick-littered, relying much more on the tried and tested. This is a performance that, despite the offbeat, shape-shifting employed by the rhythm section, never seriously considers itself on anything other than safe, familiar territory.

7

Contrary to first impressions, *Charles Mingus Presents Charles Mingus* is a studio recording. The mock-up is not intended to fool us. I do not believe Mingus wanted us to believe we are listening to a live performance. The point was not to reproduce a live sound—a gig sound. Mingus's pronouncements between tunes bring the album closer to lecture than gig. As has been pointed out by Washington and Scott Saul, the announcements are not the only factor that contributes to the album's "live" feel. Saul points to the loosening of the compositions and forms, the authenticity of the polyphony between musicians, the "slightly staggered" lack of synchronicity of Eric Dolphy (here on bass clarinet) and Ted Curson (on trumpet). He also mentions the soloing: "Curson is blurting out a solo that hitches, stumbles, and shambles forward at breakneck speed."[12] And of course there are the inflammatory lyrics—which, on paper, do not really do justice to the denunciations, taunts, cheerleading, and calls and response that form a significant part. What I find most interesting about these comparisons between the two versions is that the later, candid recording is considered a more faithful presentation of jazz work performance because of its perceived imperfection, its partiality, and its seeming like a work in progress.

8

In 2007 a long-lost recording of a 1964 performance by a Mingus combo at Cornell University in Ithaca, New York, was released.[13] This concert, from March, was among the first in a run of gigs that year that included a major European tour. There are several live recordings of "Fables" from this period.

On this (genuinely) live performance of "Fables" we hear the band stretch out even more than the live mock-up on *Charles Mingus Presents*. The piece unfolds over nearly half an hour (as was the case for all the Mingus live performances from 1964 that we have recordings of). The tune, even at this pretour stage, had been much played. The further we get from *Mingus Ah Um*, the further the performance gets from the European work-thing ideal. It is not smooth. The demeanor is positively scruffy. The now well-rehearsed head is taken at an aggressive pace, with the residue of "buttery" accord that characterized the *Mingus Ah Um* version firmly buried—precision and care is traded for immediacy and close-quarters interaction. The bridge respite is played impatiently (at a much faster speed than we hear on both studio versions I have discussed); carelessly layered minor-second intervals played by the horns suggest they are bored, as if the group is eager to get back to the issue at hand, although the forced sentimentality of the studio recordings is completely dispensed with anyhow. The comping, not limited to drums and bass, is alternatively intrusive and near nonexistent (and many points between). Solos, as in both studio versions, are fragmented, with little internal linear progression. In the Cornell performance, perhaps to a greater degree than is heard in the earlier versions, solos are not allowed the autonomy to develop their own logic (if indeed they had wanted to). On one hand, improvised shout choruses mushroom into major sections, and the soloist is swept along, regardless of where he had hoped to take the piece. On the other hand, the absence of time-constraining media allows for more expansive soundscapes to emerge from the solos and their accompaniment.[14]

If we put to one side the fact that the Cornell performance comes to us as a recording, we can point to significant disparity between the jazz studio recording and live jazz. It would be going too far to say that records completely forfeit what is central to the music's essence—that is, its partialness, incompletion, imperfection—but it is hard to deny that the jazz record brings it closer to the reification of artistic work we find in the modern European ideal.

9

I would like to return just once more to Ralph Ellison's invisible man, tucked away in his basement, enjoying his sloe gin and ice cream, and fulfilling his wish to hear five versions of "Black and Blue" played all at once; to that chance sounding together of Billie Holiday and Ornette Coleman that I spoke of in Chapter 4; to the gathering of the "Body and Soul" chorus, a disparate group of performances by Betty Carter, Archie Shepp, Dexter Gordon, and Eddie Jefferson, to name a few; and to Adorno's "satanic symphony": six records "integrated into one mighty jazz piece."[15] These are all ensembles of recordings, collections of records—record collections. A receptive listener—one whose "actions and thoughts" are arranged to be susceptible, acutely focused or absentmindedly so—might become a co-collaborator who gathers disparate performances that participate in evolving pieces or nodes of significance.[16] Record collections are dwellings of jazz work—observant of the movement of contribution. A record collection cackles with the potential of a host of incessantly reforming constellations; it holds within it a multitude of heterophonic choruses, and, in this way, it shows us the work of jazz.[17] Jazz collections are truly indispensable.

NOTES

INTRODUCTION

1. Charles Mingus Sextet with Eric Dolphy, "Fables of Faubus," on *Cornell 1964*, Blue Note 0946 3 92210 2 8, 2007 [1964], compact disc.

2. Theodor W. Adorno, *Negative Dialectics*, trans. E. B. Ashton (London: Routledge, 1973), 365.

3. Theodor W. Adorno, *Aesthetic Theory*, trans. Christian Lenhardt (London: Routledge, 1984), 207. Lenhardt's translation makes the point clearly. Here is how Robert Hullot-Kentor translated it: "It is the nonviolent synthesis of the diffuse that nevertheless preserves it as what it is in its divergences and contradictions, and for this reason form is actually an unfolding of truth. A posited unity, it constantly suspends itself as such; essential to it is that it interrupts itself through its other just as the essence of its coherence is that it does not cohere." Theodor W. Adorno, *Aesthetic Theory*, trans. Robert Hullot-Kentor (Minneapolis: University of Minnesota Press, 1997), 143. I have used Hullot-Kentor's more recent translation in most quotations drawn from *Aesthetic Theory*.

4. "Marissa Janae Johnson Speaks: #BLM, Sanders & White Progressives™ | #TWIBnation," YouTube video, 26:07, on *This Week in Blackness*, posted by "Blackness.TV | #TWIBnation," August 10, 2015, www.youtube.com/watch?v=fQqdNF-BHTw.

5. David Marriott, *Haunted Life: Visual Culture and Black Modernity* (New Brunswick, NJ: Rutgers University Press, 2007), xi. The remarks that appear at the end of this paragraph were enabled by Marriott's haunting rumination on voyeurism, record, memory, and blackness. It is a response rather than a reiteration.

6. The phrase "household of humanity" comes from Walter Benjamin, "The Storyteller: Reflections on the Works of Nikolai Leskov," in *Illuminations: Essays and Reflections* (London: Fontana, 1992), 100.

7. Even here, however, it appears in a flash, appearing to light up then extinguish quickly (perhaps in the time it takes for our cognitive faculties to kick into gear).

8. Hortense J. Spillers, "Moving On Down the Line: Variations on the African-American Sermon," in *Black, White, and in Color: Essays on American Literature and Culture* (Chicago: University of Chicago Press, 2003), 262.

9. Albrecht Wellmer, "Truth, Semblance, Reconciliation: Adorno's Aesthetic Redemption of Modernity," in *The Frankfurt School: Critical Assessments*, ed. Jay Bernstein (London: Routledge, 1994), 4:36. The latter two short quotations are from Adorno but are referenced from this essay by Wellmer. For context, as well as Wellmer's excellent essay, see Adorno, *Aesthetic Theory*, trans. Hullot-Kentor, 245.

10. The word *jazz* is used throughout this study with deep misgivings about its suitability. Should a word that may have first meant "unnecessary, misleading, or excessive talk; nonsense, rubbish . . . unnecessary ornamentation," one marred with connotations of illicit sex, be maintained? I considered following the lead of musicians such as Duke Ellington and members of the Art Ensemble of Chicago, who eschew the heavily loaded term in favor of others reflective of the heterogeneous nature of the music and also capable of highlighting the sociohistorical specificity of its emergence. But a label that specifies the blackness of jazz would require discussions that would have taken me away from my central concern. It might be argued that this book lays the groundwork for such ruminations. Also, perhaps, in light of discussions contained in this book, it is appropriate to retain a word that exemplifies the imaging of "the black"—all sweaty physicality and lacking in respectability. I have settled on the contentious but broadly accepted term, although my reluctance should be kept in mind. *Oxford English Dictionary Online*, s.v. "jazz," www.oed.com/viewdictionaryentry/Entry/100938.

11. Adorno, *Aesthetic Theory*, trans. Hullot-Kentor, 5.

12. Adorno's pronouncement that "peace is the state of differentiation without domination, with the differentiated participating in each other," allows me to speculate on whether acts of refusal of the irresistible demand to "join in" in the world may well constitute a utopia of sorts. See Theodor W. Adorno, "On Subject and Object," in *Critical Models: Interventions and Catchwords*, trans. Henry W. Pickford (New York: Columbia University Press, 2005), esp. 247. For an overview of this hook, to not "join in," see Adorno, *Problems of Moral Philosophy* (Cambridge: Polity, 2001), 167–70. See also aphorism 18, "Refuge for the Homeless," in Adorno, *Minima Moralia: Reflections on a Damaged Life*, trans. E. F. N. Jephcott (London: Verso, 2005), 38–39.

13. Krin Gabbard, "Signifyin(g) the Phallus: *Mo' Better Blues* and Representations of Jazz Trumpet," in *Representing Jazz*, ed. Krin Gabbard (Durham, NC: Duke University Press, 1995), 105.

14. Theodor W. Adorno, "On Jazz," trans. Jamie Owen Daniel, *Discourse* 12, no. 1 (1989–90): 45–69; Theodor W. Adorno, "The Perennial Fashion—Jazz," in *The Adorno Reader*, ed. Brian O'Connor (Oxford: Blackwell, 2000), 267–79. Both essays can be found in Theodor W. Adorno, *Essays on Music*, selected, with introduction, commentary, and notes, by Richard Leppert, trans. Susan H. Gillespie (Berkeley: University of California Press, 2002), 391–436, 288–317.

15. Robert W. Witkin, *Adorno on Music* (London: Routledge, 1998), 161. James Buhler argues that Adorno *was* attuned to the potential of the African American dis-

tinction from which the music originated but that he thought the ease with which it is put to use by the culture industry robs the form of its potential for mounting a challenge. Echoing Witkin, Buhler points to the fact that Adorno was often speaking of music's construction in the mainstream imagination, its "composite image . . . being proffered by the culture industry." See James Buhler, "Frankfurt School Blues: Rethinking Adorno's Critique of Jazz," in *Apparitions: New Perspectives on Adorno and Twentieth-Century Music*, ed. Berthold Hoeckner (New York: Routledge, 2006), 122. See also Robert W. Witkin, "Why Did Adorno 'Hate' Jazz?" *Sociological Theory* 18, no. 1 (2000): 145–70.

16. On "No-Such-Place" see Nathaniel Mackey, "Song of the Andoumboulou: 24," in *Whatsaid Serif* (San Francisco: City Lights, 1998), 43; Jared Sexton, "Ante-Anti-Blackness: Afterthoughts," *Lateral* 1 (2012): par. 17, https://circuitdebater.wikispaces.com/file/view/ante-anti-blackness-+afterthoughts.pdf; and Fred Moten, "Blackness and Nothingness (Mysticism in the Flesh)," *South Atlantic Quarterly* 112, no. 4 (2013): 739.

17. For a thoroughgoing history, ethnography, and discussion of the AACM see George Lewis's excellent *A Power Stronger Than Itself: The AACM and American Experimental Music* (Chicago: University of Chicago Press, 2008).

18. "AACM Panel Discussion," YouTube video, 15:00, from a panel discussion that took place at the Center for Computer Research in Music and Acoustics (CCRMA), Stanford, May 12, 2014, with Muhal Richard Abrams, Frederick Berry, George Lewis, and Roscoe Mitchell, with moderator Charles Kronengold, posted by "ccrmalite1," July 3, 2014, www.youtube.com/watch?v=HuT8r8D0w3Q.

19. Theodor Adorno and Max Horkheimer, *Towards a New Manifesto* (London: Verso, 2011), 50.

20. Vijay Iyer, "Exploding the Narrative in Jazz Improvisation," in *Uptown Conversation: The New Jazz Studies*, ed. Robert G. O'Meally, Brent Hayes Edwards, and Farah Jasmine Griffin (New York: Columbia University Press, 2004), 395.

21. Stephen Henderson, *Understanding the New Black Poetry: Black Speech and Black Music as Poetic References* (New York: William Morrow, 1973), 44.

22. Ethel Waters and Clarence Williams, "West End Blues," Columbia 14365-D, 1928, 10″; Thelonious Monk, "Monk's Mood," *Genius of Modern Music*: Vol. 2, Blue Note 4971832, 1998 [1956], compact disc.

23. Nathaniel Mackey performs this work with such virtuosity in his serial novel *From a Broken Bottle Traces of Perfume Still Emanate*. The node of significance of *mine* and *be mine* was explored in the serial's second volume, *Djbot Baghostus's Run* (Los Angeles: Sun and Moon, 1993), 59–70. As part of a recent lecture-performance at the New Museum in New York entitled "Fred Moten on Chris Ofili: Bluets, Black + Blue, In Lovely Blue," Fred Moten played an extract from artist Ben Hall's "multi-stereophonic schmear," an audio installation that augments and redepositions the work begun by *Invisible Man*. "Fred Moten on Chris Ofili: Bluets, Black + Blue, In Lovely Blue," YouTube video, 1:43:40 ("multi-stereophonic schmear" at 15:36), presented Jan. 29, 2015, posted by "New Museum," Nov. 30, 2015, www.youtube.com/watch?v=04aEVHhIVTw.

24. Aimé Césaire, Député for Martinique, to Maurice Thorez, Secretary General of

the French Communist Party, Oct. 1956, quoted in Robin D. G. Kelley's introduction to Césaire's *Discourse on Colonialism* (New York: Monthly Review Press, 2000), 25–26.

CHAPTER 1

1. Davis W. Houck and Matthew A. Grind, *Emmett Till and the Mississippi Press* (Jackson: University Press of Mississippi, 2007), 20.

2. Theodor W. Adorno, "On Jazz," trans. Jamie Owen Daniel, *Discourse* 12, no. 1 (1989–90): 67.

3. Craig Hansen Werner, *Playing the Changes: From Afro-Modernism to the Jazz Impulse* (Urbana: University of Illinois Press, 1994), 191.

4. Theodor W. Adorno, *Minima Moralia: Reflections on a Damaged Life* (London: Verso, 2005), 108.

5. Traditional class divisions no longer held as the working class and the bourgeoisie became amalgamated, corrupting and eventually rendering superfluous class consciousness. This, in part, explains Adorno's focus on consumption and the culture industry rather than production. But see Jamie Owen Daniel's (2001) essay "Achieving Subjectlessness: Reassessing the Politics of Adorno's Subject of Modernity" for an interrogation of this (http://clogic.eserver.org/3-1&2/daniel.html).

6. György Márkus, "Adorno and Mass Culture: Autonomous Art Against the Culture Industry," *Thesis Eleven* 86, no. 1 (2006): 76.

7. Theodor W. Adorno, "Freudian Theory and the Pattern of Fascist Propaganda," in *The Culture Industry: Selected Essays on Mass Culture*, ed. J. M. Bernstein (London: Routledge, 2001), 139.

8. Deborah Cook, *The Culture Industry Revisited: Theodor W. Adorno on Mass Culture* (Lanham, MD: Rowman and Littlefield, 1996), 9. Cook is quoting from the original German text: Theodor W. Adorno, "Die revidierte Psychoanalyse," in *Soziologische Schriften I* (Frankfurt am Main: Suhrkamp, 1972), 35–36.

9. "Jazz Is America" was the title of an essay by critic Marshall Stearns that appeared in the program for the 1955 Newport Jazz Festival.

10. In a much-needed reappraisal of Panassié's legacy, Tom Perchard has suggested that the emotive, first-person prose can be read as an attempt to present the music in terms that more usefully reflect the ways in which the music eludes traditional music analysis. See Tom Perchard, "Tradition, Modernity and the Supernatural Swing: Re-reading Primitivism in Hugues Panassié's Writing on Jazz," *Popular Music* 30, no. 1 (2011): 25–45.

11. Robert Goffin, "The Best Negro Jazz Orchestras," in *Beckett in Black and Red: The Translations for Nancy Cunard's "Negro" (1934)*, ed. Alan Warren Friedman (Lexington: University Press of Kentucky, 2000), 5. David Stein's essay "Negotiating Primitivist Modernisms: Louis Armstrong, Robert Goffin, and the Transatlantic Jazz Debate," *European Journal of American Studies* 6, no. 2 (2011): 1–15, is interesting, not only in its showing how Goffin edited Armstrong's memoir to fit how the musician appears in the writer's imagination but also for showing the equivocal nature of the black vernacular.

12. Goffin, "Best Negro Jazz Orchestras," 5–6.

13. Hugues Panassié, *Hot Jazz* (London: Cassell, 1936), 7.

14. Willis Conover quoted in Iain Anderson, *This Is Our Music: Free Jazz, the Sixties, and American Culture* (Philadelphia: University of Pennsylvania Press, 2007), 43.

15. Gary Giddins, *Visions of Jazz: The First Century* (Oxford: Oxford University Press, 1998), 8.

16. Goffin also recognizes a "democratic spirit" in jazz and seems to suggest that jazz has preempted political and social developments. In *Jazz: From the Congo to the Metropolitan*, trans. Walter Schaap and Leonard Feather (1944; Cambridge, MA: Da Capo, 1975), he writes: "The history of jazz has a social significance of which I am quite aware and which I am fond of stressing. At the very moment when America goes to war to defend the democratic spirit against the totalitarian challenge, it is fitting to remember that, in the last twenty years, jazz has done more to bring blacks and whites together than three amendments to the Constitution have done in seventy-five" (1).

17. John A. Kouwenhoven, *Made in America: The Arts in Modern Civilization* (Garden City, NY: Doubleday, 1948), 264. Also, in the program for the 1956 Newport Jazz Festival, Rep. Frank Thompson Jr. writes: "The way jazz works is exactly the way a democracy works. In democracy, we have complete freedom within a previously and mutually agreed upon framework of laws; in jazz, there is complete freedom within a previously and mutually agreed upon framework of tempo, key, and harmonic progression." Scott Saul, *Freedom Is, Freedom Ain't: Jazz and the Making of the Sixties* (Cambridge, MA: Harvard University Press, 2003), 15.

18. John A. Kouwenhoven, "What's 'American' About America," in *The Jazz Cadence of American Culture*, ed. Robert G. O'Meally (New York: Columbia University Press, 1998), 28. The Cold War rhetoric is strong, with Kouwenhoven defending capitalist industrial work that is set "in contrast with Charlie Chaplin's wonderful but wild fantasy of the assembly line" (134). The emphasis on the supposed isolation of musicians is also made by Marshall Stearns, who, quoting a German jazz fan, wrote that a "jam-session is a miniature democracy: every instrument is on its own and equal. The binding element is toleration and consideration for the other players." Marshall Stearns, *Altoona (PA) Tribune*, August 10, 1956, www.newspapers.com/newspage/57846467/.

19. Ralph Ellison, "The Charlie Christian Story," in *Shadow and Act* (New York: Vintage International, 1995), 234. The "assertion within and against the group" that Ellison writes about can be read as both (1) the intramural struggle for difference—that is, the tussle within the jazz ensemble or within the black community for distinction (which needs to be understood as also outward-facing, speaking to the extramural audience—"we too can be differentiated and complex") and (2) the tension between the black community and the American mainstream.

20. See the lead chapter in Michael Magee, *Emancipating Pragmatism: Emerson, Jazz, and Experimental Writing* (Tuscaloosa: University of Alabama Press, 2004).

21. Ibid., 3.

22. John Dewey, "The Live Creature and 'Ethereal Things,'" in *The Later Works of John Dewey, 1925–1953*, ed. Jo Ann Boydston, vol. 10: 1934, *Art as Experience* (Carbondale: Southern Illinois University Press, 2008), 29.

23. George Lipsitz, "Songs of the Unsung: The Darby Hicks History of Jazz," in

Uptown Conversation: The New Jazz Studies, ed. Robert G. O'Meally, Brent Hayes Edwards, and Farah Jasmine Griffin (New York: Columbia University Press, 2004), 14.

24. This is reminiscent of a line from the documentary film *The Cry of Jazz* (at 5:31): "a chain around the spirit and is a reflection of the denial of a future to the Negro in the American way of life." *The Cry of Jazz*, dir. Ed Bland (Chicago: KHTB Productions, 1959), https://youtu.be/_RAMF9X3JFc?t=5m31s.

25. Adorno, "On Jazz," 48. Daniel's claim that " 'Über Jazz' is not really 'about' its purported subject—is not about jazz as such, but rather about what its commercial production and consumption in the Europe of the 1930s represent," is misleading (Jamie Owen Daniel, "Introduction to 'On Jazz,' " *Discourse* 12, no. 1 [1989–90]: 39–40). It is true that jazz is positioned from the outset as a part of the culture industry and, according to Adorno, is unqualified to receive sustained musical analysis. But Adorno spends a good portion of the essay addressing what he considers the music's most important musical components. When he informs us that understanding jazz works does not require "questions like those pertaining to the autonomous work of art," he attempts to legitimize an approach that bypasses sustained analysis but nonetheless engages poorly formed ideas concerning the music to support the case being brought against it.

26. Adorno, "On Jazz," 68.

27. Ibid., 56.

28. Ibid., 54.

29. Theodore Gracyk, "Adorno, Jazz, and the Aesthetics of Popular Music," *Musical Quarterly* 76, no. 4 (1992): 538.

30. A common complaint leveled at his jazz critique is that Adorno just did not understand the music. Wolfgang Sandner goes so far as to claim that Adorno had given up listening to jazz after the mid-1930s "without . . . giving up writing about it." Sandner is quoted in Max Paddison, "The Critique Criticised: Adorno and Popular Music," *Popular Music* 2 (1982): 210. Alongside this charge of ignorance are more serious allegations, including those of elitism and, less often, racism. For Lorenzo Thomas, Adorno's contribution in highlighting marketing's degradation of music is compromised by his "total inability to recognize blacks . . . as people capable of creating a self-conscious and original art." See Lorenzo Thomas, *Don't Deny My Name: Words and Music and the Black Intellectual Tradition* (Ann Arbor: University of Michigan Press, 2008), 106. In agreement with Adorno's critics, contributors on the other side of the fence also point to his lack of exposure to "genuine" jazz and argue that the music he was referring to "has little to do with the richness of a Black culture we have only long since then discovered." Fredric Jameson, *Late Marxism: Adorno, or the Persistence of the Dialectic* (London: Verso, 2007), 141. Jameson's suggestion that Adorno was referring to commercial swing bands rather than the "hot bands" we most often associate with black musicians does have some truth to it. Adorno makes clear, however, that he recognized the stylistic difference between bebop and swing and that he had, in fact, heard Louis Armstrong and Duke Ellington, two musicians whose contributions are widely considered quintessential "black music." Evelyn Wilcock substantiates this, pointing out that Adorno would have had to try hard to avoid "black jazz" during his time as a doctoral student at Oxford University

(incidentally, when and where he wrote "Über Jazz"). See Evelyn Wilcock, "Adorno, Jazz and Racism: 'Über Jazz' and the 1934–7 British Jazz Debate," *Telos* 107 (1996): 63–80. Yet all of this may be inconsequential. As Richard Leppert points out, Adorno believed that whether referring to the "dance-band commercial" variety or "Negro jazz . . . , there is nothing to salvage" from either because "jazz itself has long been in the process of dissolution." See Theodor W. Adorno, *Essays on Music*, selected, with introduction, commentary, and notes, by Richard Leppert, trans. Susan H. Gillespie (Berkeley: University of California Press, 2002), 359.

31. Adorno, "On Jazz," 66.

32. There is real confusion about what subject is being referred to at various points in "Über Jazz." Susan Buck-Morss, in *The Origin of Negative Dialectics: Theodor W. Adorno, Walter Benjamin, and the Frankfurt Institute* (New York: Free Press, 1977), takes the "jazz subject" to refer to the jazz musician whereas others, such as Daniel, in her introduction to "On Jazz," seem to interpret it as the (bourgeois or mass) consumer. This, I believe, is a theoretical device as well as a rhetorical one for Adorno. (I do not believe that it is mere carelessness.) It supports Adorno's contention that, ultimately, we all belong to a "universal class" and that our existence in late capitalism can be encapsulated by that of the bourgeoisie. (There may be confusion at certain times about who is being referred to, but there is no mistaking that this is a chapter in Adorno's story of the disenfranchisement of the bourgeoisie.) This vagueness has interesting implications when Adorno talks of castration, clowns, and slaves and especially when we are told of "oppressed people" being particularly well-adapted for jazz and life under monopolized capitalism. We find implied in the text that the African American experience plays out in advance that which is taking hold of the modern mainstream.

I am of the opinion that the "jazz subject" of Adorno's essays wavers between the musician, the bourgeois, and a "mass class." But the "hot subject" appears to refer uncontestably to the jazz musician. And for those who believe that Adorno only knew of white bands and musicians, even in "On Jazz"—where he all but denies the black basis of jazz—he tells us that the music is "frequently performed by blacks" (52). See also Wilcock, "Adorno, Jazz and Racism," 10. This point gains significance when I come to address the default address of black subjectivity within that of the bourgeoisie.

33. Adorno, "On Jazz," 64–65, 67.

34. Theodor W. Adorno, "Culture Industry Reconsidered," trans. Anson G. Rabinbach, *New German Critique*, no. 6 (Fall 1975): 18–19.

35. Cook, *The Culture Industry Revisited*, 9.

36. Theodor W. Adorno and Joachim-Ernst Berendt, "Pro and Contra Jazz," *German History in Documents and Images* 8 (1953): 3, http://germanhistorydocs.ghi-dc.org/pdf/eng/Vol.8_Chap.27_Doc.05_ENGL.pdf.

37. "The actual consciousness of the actual proletariat . . . ha[s] nothing, absolutely nothing, over the bourgeoisie except for an interest in the revolution, but who otherwise bear all the marks of the bourgeoisie's truncated personality." Adorno to Walter Benjamin, quoted in Buck-Morss, *The Origin of Negative Dialectics*, 30.

38. Theodor W. Adorno, "On the Social Situation of Music," in *Essays on Music*, se-

lected, with introduction, commentary, and notes, by Richard Leppert, trans. Susan H. Gillespie (Berkeley: University of California Press, 2002), 427.

39. Adorno quoted in Max Paddison, *Adorno's Aesthetics of Music* (Cambridge: Cambridge University Press, 1993), 118. Paddison's translation is modified from that of Wes Blomster's 1978 version reproduced in Richard Leppert's edition of Adorno's *Essays on Music.*

40. Paddison, *Adorno's Aesthetics*, 118 (emphasis added).

41. Daniel, "Achieving Subjectlessness," point 25.

42. Adorno, "On Jazz," 52.

43. Theodor W. Adorno, "The Perennial Fashion—Jazz," in *The Adorno Reader*, ed. Brian O'Connor (Oxford: Blackwell, 2000), 269.

44. Ibid.

45. Theodor W. Adorno, *Introduction to the Sociology of Music* (New York: Continuum, 1988), 57.

46. Adorno, "The Perennial Fashion—Jazz," 275, 278.

47. Fred Moten, *In the Break: The Aesthetics of the Black Radical Tradition* (Minneapolis: University of Minnesota Press, 2003), 179.

48. The denial of the slave's parental privilege, and the persisting repercussions of this, is well documented. Wilma A. Dunaway, writing of slave families in Appalachia, states, "In the Upper South states, one in every three slave marriages was broken by a master's intervention. One in every three slave marriages was terminated when masters sold spouses away from their families. Moreover, one-half of all slave sales involved the separation of children from their parents." Since children were regarded as the property of their mother's owner, any "kinship interaction" with their fathers was at the behest of those owners. Dunaway reveals that fathers, whether absent or no, were often a secondary influence on their children at best, with the slaveholder exercising ultimate paternal privilege. Wilma A. Dunaway, *The African-American Family in Slavery and Emancipation* (Cambridge: Cambridge University Press, 2003), 63.

At the root of this legacy we find the portrait of a patriarchal slaveholder who installed himself as the universal disciplinarian—"paterfamilias" to both his white family and to the slaves he owned. Eugene D. Genovese, *Roll, Jordan, Roll: The World the Slaves Made* (New York: Pantheon, 1974), 483. In the absence of the authority of biological parents, the slave child was held "under the press of a patronymic, patrifocal, patrilineal, and patriarchal order." Hortense J. Spillers, " 'Mama's Baby, Papa's Maybe: American Grammar Book," in *Black, White, and in Color: Essays on American Literature and Culture* (Chicago: University of Chicago Press, 2003), 218.

49. This fettering of the black psyche, as Sylvia Hewlett and Cornel West tell us, "utterly demolished the male protector/provider role and the pride, dignity, and strength that came with it." Sylvia A. Hewlett and Cornel West, *The War Against Parents: What We Can Do for America's Beleaguered Moms and Dads* (Boston: Mariner, 1998), 181. Unlike the modern bourgeoisie or "universal class," no myth of individuality or personal distinction is afforded the black slave. For the female slave, "the alleged benefits of the ideology of feminity [*sic*] did not accrue. . . . She was not sheltered or protected; she

would not remain oblivious to the desperate struggle for existence unfolding outside the 'home.' She was also there in the fields, alongside the man, toiling under the lash from sun-up to sun-down." Angela Davis, "Reflections on the Black Woman's Role in the Community of Slaves," in *Words of Fire: An Anthology of African-American Feminist Thought*, ed. Beverly Guy-Sheftall (New York: New Press, 1995), 205. Also see Saidiya Hartman, *Scenes of Subjection: Terror, Slavery, and Self-Making in Nineteenth-Century America* (New York: Oxford University Press, 1997).

50. Adorno wrote, "Hitler posed as a composite of King Kong and the suburban barber" to emphasize the everyday quality of the totalitarian. See Adorno, "Freudian Theory," 141.

51. Hortense J. Spillers, " 'All the Things You Could Be by Now, If Sigmund Freud's Wife Was Your Mother': Psychoanalysis and Race," in *Black, White, and in Color: Essays on American Literature and Culture* (Chicago: University of Chicago Press, 2003), 395.

52. Frantz Fanon, *Black Skin, White Masks* (London: Pluto, 2008), 82–86.

53. W. E. B. Du Bois, *The Souls of Black Folk* (New York: Dover, 1994), 2. Du Bois's formulation of "double consciousness" and its various extrapolations is explored in Chapter 2.

54. Theodor W. Adorno, *Negative Dialectics*, trans. E. B. Ashton (London: Routledge, 1973), 6.

55. Adorno, "On Jazz," 64.

56. Still, even in 1936 swing, the verse of the verse-refrain form is often dropped in performance and recording.

57. Adorno, "On Jazz," 64–65.

58. Stephen Henderson, *Understanding the New Black Poetry: Black Speech and Black Music as Poetic References* (New York: Morrow, 1973), 44 (emphasis in original).

59. Ralph Ellison, "The Seer and the Seen," in *Shadow and Act* (New York: Vintage International, 1995), 78.

60. It is interesting that the "song form" that is often contained in jazz is neglected in Adorno's analysis. AABA is suggestive of two distinct voices involved in dialogue rather than the absorption of the initiating theme into the second.

61. Susan McClary, *Conventional Wisdom: The Content of Musical Form* (Berkeley: University of California Press, 2000), 39.

62. See Chapter 4 for more on this.

63. "As John Coltrane once said, the audience heard 'We' even if the singer said 'I' " (McClary, *Conventional Wisdom*, 47).

64. Ellison, "The Seer and the Seen," 78.

CHAPTER 2

1. Theodor W. Adorno, "On Jazz," trans. Jamie Owen Daniel, *Discourse* 12, no. 1 (1989–90): 48.

2. My meaning here is similar to that of both James Martin Harding and Fredric Jameson, who point to Adorno's alleged lack of exposure to jazz of the African American variety. See James Martin Harding, "Adorno, Ellison, and the Critique of Jazz," *Cultural*

Critique 31 (1995): 129–58; and Fredric Jameson, *Late Marxism: Adorno, or the Persistence of the Dialectic* (London: Verso, 2007), 141.

3. W. E. B. Du Bois, *The Souls of Black Folk* (New York: Dover, 1994), 2.

4. Hortense J. Spillers, "The Idea of Black Culture," *CR: The New Centennial Review* 6, no. 3 (2006): 26.

5. Adorno, "On Jazz," 53.

6. Theodor W. Adorno, "On the Social Situation of Music," in *Essays on Music*, selected, with introduction, commentary, and notes, by Richard Leppert, trans. Susan H. Gillespie (Berkeley: University of California Press, 2002), 427–28 (emphasis mine).

7. Ibid., 391.

8. Ibid.

9. Adorno uses this term in a response to Walter Benjamin's "The Work of Art in the Age of Mechanical Reproduction." In this seminal essay Benjamin mourns the loss of aura in high art, while showing great enthusiasm for new modes of mass reproduction such as cinema. Adorno, in a letter written in 1936, the year "Über Jazz" was published, writes to Benjamin: "Both bear the stigmata of capitalism, both contain elements of change. . . . Both are torn halves of an integral freedom, to which, however, they do not add up. It would be romantic to sacrifice one to the other." Theodor W. Adorno and Walter Benjamin, *The Complete Correspondence, 1928–40*, ed. Henri Lonitz, trans. Nicholas Walker (Cambridge, MA: Harvard University Press, 1999), 130. Adorno's discussion of art and light music in "On the Social Situation of Music" uses a very similar formulation.

In this period, art is "bourgeois" owing to its audience, the ability of the artist to function within market capitalism, and, perhaps most importantly, because of its being a "portrayal of bourgeois self-understanding." Peter Burger, *Theory of the Avant-Garde* (Manchester: Manchester University Press, 1984), 48.

10. Theodor W. Adorno, *Aesthetic Theory*, trans. Robert Hullot-Kentor (Minneapolis: University of Minnesota Press, 1997), 252.

11. Max Paddison, *Adorno's Aesthetics of Music* (Cambridge: Cambridge University Press, 1993), 220–21.

12. Andrew Hamilton, "Adorno and the Autonomy of Art," in *Nostalgia for a Redeemed Future: Critical Theory*, ed. Stefano G. Ludovisi and Agostini G. Saavedra (Rome: John Cabot University Press, 2009), 257.

13. Robert W. Witkin, *Adorno on Music* (London: Routledge, 1988), 12; Lambert Zuidervaart, "The Social Significance of Autonomous Art: Adorno and Bürger," *Journal of Aesthetics and Art Criticism* 48, no. 1 (1990): 61–77.

14. Adorno, "Social Situation of Music," 393. For Adorno the functional distance required for such insight bars music's direct involvement in extramusical institutions and forms of communication. The passivity of such an enterprise is not lost on Adorno. Neither is its obstruction, not only to the revolutionary commitment of more politically inclined Marxist aestheticians such as Hanns Eisler but also, to a certain extent, Adorno's own utopian hope for a "true collective" that would embody a more empathetic way of being with others. See Susan Buck-Morss, *The Origin of Negative Dialectics: Theodor W. Adorno, Walter Benjamin, and the Frankfurt Institute* (New York: Free Press, 1977), 42.

15. Theodor W. Adorno, *Philosophy of Modern Music* (London: A&C Black, 2003), 36n5.

16. The narrator had just been expelled from college owing to a series of events in which he allowed a white trustee of the college to trespass on the "communal underground." There they encountered tales of inadvertent incest and a riot at the asylum/tavern but, most damningly, according to the narrator, a violation by the doctor-patient of the accepted conventions of interracial conduct.

17. Ellison, *Invisible Man*, 154.

18. Edward M. Pavlić, *Crossroads Modernism: Descent and Emergence in African-American Literary Culture* (Minneapolis: University of Minnesota Press, 2002), 82. According to Pavlić, a key feature of this is that "syndetic cultural patterns resist the stable and ordering influences of modern rationalisations" (22). See also James Snead's provocative reading of Hegel's dismissal of the possibility of African subjecthood in "On Repetition in Black Culture," *Black American Literature Forum* 15, no. 4 (1981): 148–49.

19. Ellison, *Invisible Man*, 154.

20. W. E. B. Du Bois, "Of the Passing of the First-Born," in *The Souls of Black Folk* (1903; New York: Dover, 1994), 128:

> And thus in the Land of the Color-line I saw, as it fell across my baby, the shadow of the Veil.
>
> Within the Veil was he born, said I; and there within shall he live,—a Negro and a Negro's son. Holding in that little head—ah, bitterly!—the unbowed pride of a hunted race, clinging with that tiny dimpled hand—ah, wearily!—to a hope not hopeless but unhopeful, and seeing with those bright wondering eyes that peer into my soul a land whose freedom is to us a mockery and whose liberty a lie.

21. W. E. B. Du Bois, "Beyond the Veil in a Virginia Town (1897)," in *Against Racism: Unpublished Essays, Papers, Addresses, 1887–1961*, ed. Herbert Aptheker (Amherst: University of Massachusetts Press, 1988), 50.

22. Nahum D. Chandler, "Of Horizon: An Introduction to 'The Afro-American' by W. E. B. Du Bois—circa 1894," *Journal of Transnational American Studies* 2, no. 1 (2010): 17 (emphasis in original).

23. Lorenzo Thomas, *Don't Deny My Name: Words and Music and the Black Intellectual Tradition* (Ann Arbor: University of Michigan Press, 2008), 105; Bob Kaufman, "Battle Report," in *Solitudes Crowded with Loneliness* (New York: New Directions, 1965), 8; Bob Kaufman, "O-Jazz-O War Memoir: Jazz, Don't Listen to It at Your Own Risk," in *Cranial Guitar: Selected Poems* (Minneapolis: Coffee House Press, 1996), 96. For more on Kaufman and jazz see Lorenzo Thomas's *Don't Deny My Name* and Amor Kohli's "Saxophones and Smothered Rage: Bob Kaufman, Jazz and the Quest for Redemption," *Callaloo* 25, no. 1 (2002): 165–82.

24. Amiri Baraka, *Dutchman*, in *The LeRoi Jones/Amiri Baraka Reader*, ed. William J. Harris (New York: Thunder's Mouth, 1999), 97. The play appeared before his black nationalist period and was critically acclaimed, earning Baraka—then known as LeRoi Jones—an Obie Award for best off-Broadway play. For a dispassionate reconsideration of Baraka's gender politics from his black nationalist period, showing how gender crosses

race in his radicalism in a way that required him to propagate the "disempowerment" of black women, see Daniel Matlin's "'Lift Up Yr Self!' Reinterpreting Amiri Baraka (LeRoi Jones), Black Power, and the Uplift Tradition," *Journal of American History* 93, no. 1 (2006): 91–116. Interestingly, although approaching from a different direction, Ellison, in "The Art of Fiction: An Interview," describing the transformation that the narrator of *Invisible Man* goes through as that from "a would-be politician and rabble-rouser and orator to that of writer" (*Shadow and Act*, 76), appears to agree with Baraka's assertion that art becomes a conduit for protest. We should keep in mind, however, that Ellison rejected suggestions that the novel was a protest.

25. Dizzy Gillespie, although critical, acknowledged his influence. Quoted in a Nat Hentoff article, he says, "If it hadn't been for him, there would have been none of us. I want to thank Mr. Louis Armstrong for my livelihood." "When I Pick Up That Horn, That's All: The Life and Music of Louis Armstrong," *Gadfly*, March/April 2000, www.gadflyonline.com/archive/marchapril00/archive-louisarmstrong.html.

26. Lester Bowie quoted in Charles Hersch, "Poisoning Their Coffee: Louis Armstrong and Civil Rights," *Polity* 34, no. 3 (2002): 380.

27. All transcriptions from "The Clown" are my own. Charles Mingus, "The Clown," on *The Clown*, Rhino Records 8122-79641-5, 2013 [1957], compact disc. The narration is of a story written by Mingus and was improvised by Jean Shepherd. From Nat Hentoff's liner notes:

> The Clown has improvised narration by Jean Shepherd who at the time was active on the New York jazz [scene] and was also a truly original radio improviser—his instruments being memory, desire, and a very singular imagination that made his wordscapes unlike [*sic*] no one else's on the air.
>
> Mingus told me how The Clown had originated:
>
> "I felt happy one day. I was playing a little tune on the piano that sounded happy. Then I hit a dissonance that sounded sad, and I realized that the song had to have two parts. The story, as I told it first to Jean Shepherd, is about a clown who tried to please people—like most jazz musicians do—but whom nobody liked until he was dead. My version of the story ended with the clown's blowing his brains out, with the people laughing and finally being pleased because they thought it was part of the act. I liked the way Jean changed the ending; it leaves more up to the listener.
>
> "We rehearsed once at my house, and then did it in the studio. His narration changed every time. He improvised within the story. As for the musicians, Jimmy is the leader in this piece. We play around what he does. When we do a work in a place where we have no narration, Jimmy is the clown."

The piece has been explored as a "satirical self-portrait" by Jennifer Griffith in "Mingus in the Act: Confronting the Legacies of Vaudeville and Minstrelsy," *Jazz Perspectives* 4, no. 3 (2010): 361. See also Mario Dunkel, *Aesthetics of Resistance: Charles Mingus and the Civil Rights Movement* (Zurich: Lit Verlag, 2012).

28. Ralph Ellison, "The Seer and the Seen," in *Shadow and Act* (New York: Vintage International, 1995), 26.

29. W. E. B. Du Bois, "Of Our Spiritual Strivings," in *The Souls of Black Folk* (New York: Dover, 1994), 2.

30. See Ingrid Monson, *Saying Something: Jazz Improvisation and Interaction* (Chicago: University of Chicago Press, 1996); Ingrid Monson, "Doubleness and Jazz Improvisation: Irony, Parody, and Ethnomusicology," *Critical Inquiry* 20, no. 2 (1994): 283–313; and David Borgo, "The Play of Meaning and the Meaning of Play in Jazz," *Journal of Consciousness Studies* 11, no. 3/4 (2004): 174–90. Paul Austerlitz makes a similar attempt in his book *Jazz Consciousness: Music, Race, and Humanity* (Middletown, CT: Wesleyan University Press, 2005), although his study follows a track more faithful to the discipline of ethnomusicology.

31. Amiri Baraka, *Digging: The Afro-American Soul of American Classical Music* (Berkeley: University of California Press, 2009), 106, 36.

32. Austerlitz picks up on this ambivalence in his introduction to *Jazz Consciousness.*

33. Monson, *Saying Something*, 132.

34. Charles Hersch, *Subversive Sounds: Race and the Birth of Jazz in New Orleans* (Chicago: University of Chicago Press, 2008), 16.

35. Borgo, "The Play of Meaning," 181.

36. Monson, *Saying Something*, 100.

37. Ronald M. Radano, *Lying up a Nation: Race and Black Music* (Chicago: University of Chicago Press, 2003), 10.

38. Most often encountered in Du Bois's *The Souls of Black Folk*, an earlier version of the essay was published in 1897 in the *Atlantic Monthly*. Monson also refers to a second quotation that perhaps had greater influence on her understanding of double consciousness. This is from a posthumously published sketch of his visit to Prince Edward County, Virginia, written sometime between late 1897 and 1898. Du Bois writes: "You who live in single towns will hardly comprehend the double life of this Virginia hamlet. The doctrine of class does not explain it—the caste misses the kernel of truth. It is two worlds separate yet bound together like those double stars that, bound for all time, whirl around each other separate yet one" (Du Bois, "Beyond the Veil," 49). This appears to be the basis of Monson's consideration, and through it our attention is drawn to an isolated strand of the grand concept—that of "twoness." This sets up a discussion concerning multiple voices, dual identity, and admixture. See Monson, *Saying Something*, 98–101.

39. Double consciousness as a play of difference between the general social field and the sociality taking place behind the veil is dynamic but not "dialectic" in the strictly Hegelian sense of the term. The dogged irresolution of these conflicting positions—their conflict having less to do with incompatible racial or cultural markers than with the irreducibility of black heterogeneity on the one side and the tendency toward homogeneity on the other—results in what Chandler, borrowing from Jacques Derrida, calls "desedimentation"—that is, to "make tremble by dislodging the layers of sedimented premises that hold in place" consolidated hegemony. There is a suggestion of utopian promise inherent in the ever-present potential for loosening congealed positions of thought—a "longing to . . . merge . . . double self into a better and truer self" without giving up the distinction between the two parts.

40. Nahum D. Chandler, "Originary Displacement," *boundary 2* 27, no. 3 (2000): 258.

41. Ibid., 268.

42. Ibid., 273.

43. Ibid., 250–51. Hortense J. Spillers draws from Chandler's essay, as part of a parallel discussion concerning the necessity (or otherwise) of cultural difference: "we should think that 'black culture,' which might be established as an 'example,' might take us back or ahead to the problematic of culture in general and 'as such.'" Spillers, "The Idea of Black Culture," 25. We also see something of this in Austerlitz's *Jazz Consciousness*, a study on the music's global "inclusiveness." Austerlitz uses double consciousness as an analytical framework to think through transnational affiliations and contextual distinction.

44. Nahum D. Chandler, "Of Exorbitance: The Problem of the Negro as a Problem for Thought," *Criticism* 50, no. 3 (2008): 347.

45. Adorno, *Philosophy of Modern Music*, 26n5.

46. Theodor W. Adorno, "The Perennial Fashion—Jazz," in *The Adorno Reader*, ed. Brian O'Connor (Oxford: Blackwell, 2000), 269.

47. Adorno, "On Jazz," 47; Adorno, "The Perennial Fashion—Jazz," 269.

48. Note here the focus on divergent styles rather than industry mutilation. I would argue that whether "sweet" or "hot," the overwhelming problem is the bloodletting of blackness from above-underground transformations.

49. Joseph D. Lewandowski, "Adorno on Jazz and Society," *Philosophy and Social Criticism* 22, no. 5 (1996): 104.

50. Adorno, "The Perennial Fashion—Jazz," 269.

51. Hortense J. Spillers, "Moving On Down the Line: Variations on the African-American Sermon," in *Black, White, and in Color: Essays on American Literature and Culture* (Chicago: University of Chicago Press, 2003), 262.

52. Adorno, "The Perennial Fashion—Jazz," 268; Adorno, "On Jazz," 67, 68.

53. Mingus on "rotary perception": "With Rotary Perception you may imagine a circle round the beat. . . . The notes can fall at any point within the circle so that the original feeling for the beat is not disturbed. If anyone in the group loses confidence, one of the quartet can hit the beat again." Brian Priestley, *Mingus: A Critical Biography* (New York: Da Capo, 1983), 124–25. See also Fred Moten, "The New International of Rhythmic Feeling(s)," *Thamyris/Intersecting: Place, Sex and Race* 18, no. 1 (2008): 31–56.

54. See Moten, "The New International of Rhythmic Feeling(s)."

55. Chandler, "Originary Displacement," 275; Nahum D. Chandler, *X—The Problem of the Negro as a Problem for Thought* (New York: Fordham University Press, 2014), 121.

56. Theodor W. Adorno, *Aesthetic Theory*, trans. Robert Hullot-Kentor (Minneapolis: University of Minnesota Press, 1997), 168.

57. Ibid., 106.

58. David Jenemann, *Adorno in America* (Minneapolis: University of Minnesota Press, 2007), 114.

59. Ellison, *Invisible Man*, 8 (emphasis in original). See Alexander Weheliye's *Phonographies: Grooves in Sonic Afro-Modernity* for an inspired reading of the invisible

man's listening preferential toward a formulation of the sonic black modern (Durham, NC: Duke University Press, 2005).

60. Fred Moten, "Fred Moten on Chris Ofili: Bluets, Black + Blue, In Lovely Blue," lecture-presentation at the New Museum (NY), Jan. 29, 2015, posted by "New Museum," Nov. 30, 2015, www.youtube.com/watch?v=04aEVHhIVTw.

CHAPTER 3

1. The second half of this chapter's title is taken from the eighteenth aphorism in Theodor Adorno's *Minima Moralia: Reflections on a Damaged Life* (Verso: London, 2005), 38. It is the passage that contains what is perhaps the book's most famous sentence: "Wrong life cannot be lived rightly" (39).

2. Diane Dorr-Dorynek, "Mingus . . . ," in *The Jazz Word*, ed. Dom Cerulli, Burt Korall, and Mort L. Nasatir (New York: Ballantine, 1987), 17; Scott Saul, *Freedom Is, Freedom Ain't: Jazz and the Making of the Sixties* (Cambridge, MA: Harvard University Press, 2003), 167; Mario Dunkel, *Aesthetics of Resistance: Charles Mingus and the Civil Rights Movement* (Zurich: Lit Verlag, 2012).

3. Charles Mingus, *Beneath the Underdog* (Edinburgh: Canongate, 2011), 334.

4. This is adapted from "household of humanity." Walter Benjamin, "The Storyteller: Reflections on the Works of Nikolai Leskov," in *Illuminations: Essays and Reflections* (London: Fontana, 1992), 100.

5. Mingus quoted in Dorr-Dorynek, "Mingus . . . ," 16–18.

6. Ibid., 16. Within his improvised monologues Mingus presents insightful portrayals that call to mind Adorno's "regressive listener."

7. Mingus quoted in ibid., 18. This echoes the plea made by John Coltrane to critics: "Get all the understanding for what you're speaking of that you can get." John Coltrane quoted in Leonard L. Brown, "In His Own Words: Coltrane's Responses to Critics," in *John Coltrane and Black America's Quest for Freedom: Spirituality and the Music*, ed. Leonard L. Brown (New York: Oxford University Press, 2010), 14.

8. Cecil Taylor quoted in Eric Porter, *What Is This Thing Called Jazz? African American Musicians as Artists, Critics, and Activists* (Berkeley: University of California Press, 2002), 200; Archie Shepp, "An Artist Speaks Bluntly," *Downbeat*, Dec. 16, 1965, 42. This idea of bringing people to an understanding of blackness frames Shepp's rejection of the bourgeois ideal of autonomy within a discourse that is broader than the "black anger" narrative. It also calls to mind Amiri Baraka's "New Black Music is this: Find the self, then kill it." Amiri Baraka, *Black Music: Essays by LeRoi Jones (Amiri Baraka)* (New York: Akashic, 2010), 201.

9. See, e.g., Leonard L. Brown, ed., *John Coltrane and Black America's Quest for Freedom: Spirituality and the Music* (New York: Oxford University Press, 2010).

10. Porter, *What Is This Thing Called Jazz?* 197. Eric Porter is not alone in his interpretation of Coltrane's "universalist" approach to music as being an affront to "those who wished to limit the meaning and function of this music to an African American context." Mark Gridley argues similarly, and his research on the perceptions of anger appears to be motivated, to some extent, by a desire to cordon off an area free of social

and political (read black) context. Mark Gridley, "Misconceptions of Linking Free Jazz with the Civil Rights Movement," *College Music Symposium* 47 (2007): 139–55. Aram Sinnreich also makes a virtue of Coltrane's supposed apoliticism, writing, "Ironically, Coltrane's self-oriented meditations succeeded where Mingus's exhortative bluster had failed. Coltrane's music, despite or because of its complete absence of explicit political messaging, became a touchstone for the new black consciousness, in America and around the world." Aram Sinnreich, "All That Jazz Was: Remembering the Mainstream Avant-Garde," *American Quarterly* 57, no. 2 (2005): 568–69. The more essentialist elements of black nationalism have been well documented. Studies by Porter (*What Is This Thing Called Jazz?*), Ronald M. Radano (*New Musical Figurations: Anthony Braxton's Cultural Critique* [Chicago: University of Chicago Press, 1993]), and George Lewis (*A Power Stronger Than Itself: The AACM and American Experimental Music* [Chicago: University of Chicago Press, 2008]) are all excellent. As Porter has shown, musicians such as drummer Milford Graves, who is linked to The Black Arts Repertory Theatre/School set up by Baraka, did call for organized, collective action through a program of "intellectual, cultural, and economic self-reliance" (199).

11. "I'm trying so many things at one time. . . . I haven't sorted them out." "Interview with John Coltrane by Carl-Eric Lindgren," Stockholm, March 21, 1960, YouTube video, 1:06, posted March 19, 2015, www.youtube.com/watch?v=TdBQbu5ADhw.

12. John Coltrane quoted in Brown, "In His Own Words," 17; and John Coltrane quoted in "John Coltrane and Eric Dolphy Answer the Critics," *Downbeat*, Dec. 4, 1962. There is a similar tone of black/jazz moral responsibility in Martin Luther King's address at the 1964 Berlin Jazz Festival: "Jazz is exported to the world. For in the specific struggle of the Negro in America there is something akin to the universal struggle of modern man." Martin Luther King Jr., "Dr. Martin Luther King Jr.'s Address to the 1964 Berlin Jazz Festival," *JazzTimes*, Jan. 21, 2008, https://jazztimes.com/news/dr-martin-luther-king-jr-s-address-to-the-1964-berlin-jazz-festival/.

13. Nathaniel Mackey, "Song of the Andoumboulou: 24," in *Whatsaid Serif* (San Francisco: City Lights, 1998), 43.

14. Nathaniel Mackey, *Splay Anthem* (New York: New Directions, 2006), 5; Nathaniel Mackey, *From a Broken Bottle Traces of Perfume Still Emanate* (New York: New Directions, 2010). The formulation/phrase "post-expectant" is much used by Mackey.

15. Mackey, "Andoumboulouous Brush," in *Splay Anthem*, 6.

16. Frank B. Wilderson III, *Red, White & Black: Cinema and the Structure of U.S. Antagonisms* (Durham, NC: Duke University Press, 2010). Although Sexton often models the conversation as one between Moten and Wilderson, it is most usefully followed through the following essays: Fred Moten, "The Case of Blackness," *Criticism* 50, no. 2 (2008): 177–218; Jared Sexton, "The Social Life of Social Death: On Afro-pessimism and Black Optimism," *InTensions* 5 (2011): www.yorku.ca/intent/issue5/articles/jaredsexton.php; Fred Moten, "Blackness and Nothingness (Mysticism in the Flesh)," *South Atlantic Quarterly* 112, no. 4 (2013): 737–80. These essays present a very focused strand of dialogue within a wider debate.

17. Wilderson, *Red, White & Black*, 24. Also: "I am arguing that whereas alienation

is an essential grammar underpinning Human relationality, it is an important but ultimately inessential grammar when one attempts to think the structural interdiction against Black recognition and incorporation. In other words, alienation is a grammar underwriting all manner of relationality, whether narcissistic (egoic, empty speech) or liberated (full speech). But it is not a grammar that underwrites, much less explains, the absence of relationality" (ibid., 73).

18. Theodor W. Adorno, "On Jazz," trans. Jamie Owen Daniel, *Discourse* 12, no. 1 (1989–90): 52, 53.

19. Sexton, "Social Life of Social Death," par. 24. Listen to Sexton during the Q&A session at the end of his lecture "People-of-Color-Blindness" at the University of California, Berkeley. He recounts a gig at which Sonny Rollins's microphone had stopped working. The organizers or technicians came onto the stage to fix the problem but were berated by the drummer, who made it clear that what was important was that the band members could hear each other. Jared Sexton, "People-of-Color-Blindness: A Lecture by Jared Sexton," YouTube video, 54:06, posted by UC Berkeley Events, Oct. 27, 2011, www.youtube.com/watch?v=qNVMI3oiDaI.

20. Moten's inclination toward "life and optimism over death and pessimism," his desire that the contributions he makes weigh in at "49.99% critique and 50.01% celebration," flags him as suspect within the framework of the Afro-pessimism project. Any appeal to consolatory expressive solace falls short of the required vigilance toward complicity. Leaning on the redemptive qualities of black expression as a way to soften the harsh reality of societal impotence only assists the "diffusion of terror"—black life being dispossessed even of its own enjoyment. The phrase "diffusion of terror" is from Saidiya V. Hartman, *Scenes of Subjection: Terror, Slavery, and Self-Making in Nineteenth-Century America* (New York: Oxford University Press, 1997): "By defamiliarizing the familiar, I hope to illuminate the terror of the mundane and quotidian rather than exploit the shocking spectacle. What concerns me here is the diffusion of terror and the violence perpetrated under the rubric of pleasure, paternalism, and property" (4). See also Saidiya V. Hartman, "The Position of the Unthought," interview by Frank B. Wilderson III, *Qui Parle* 13, no. 2 (2003): 183–201.

21. See Lewis R. Gordon, *Her Majesty's Other Children: Sketches of Racism from a Neocolonial Age* (Lanham, MD: Rowman and Littlefield, 1997): "Now, recall my point about the two dominant principles of racist ideology: (1) be white, but above all, (2) don't be black. We can call the first *the principle of white supremacy*; and we can call the second *the principle of black inferiority*" (63).

22. Jared Sexton, "Ante-Anti-Blackness: Afterthoughts," *Lateral* 1 (2012), par. 17, https://circuitdebater.wikispaces.com/file/view/ante-anti-blackness-+afterthoughts.pdf; Moten, "Blackness and Nothingness," 739.

23. Fred Moten, "Blackness and Poetry," *Evening Will Come*, no. 55 (2015): sec. 1, par. 1, www.thevolta.org/ewc55-fmoten-p1.html.

24. Stefano Harney and Fred Moten, "Michael Brown," *boundary 2* 42, no. 4 (2015): 83.

25. See Stefano Harney and Fred Moten, *The Undercommons: Fugitive Planning and*

Black Study (New York: Minor Compositions, 2013), 154. See also Fred Moten's "consent not to be a single being," a short reflection published on the Poetry Foundation's website that gives a little more background and definitional depth to this recurring Motenian theme. It speaks to my discussions in Chapter 1 concerning blackness as emblematic of the unavailability and unviability of individualism in this late modern. Fred Moten, "To Consent Not to Be a Single Being," www.poetryfoundation.org/harriet/2010/02/to-consent-not-to-be-a-single-being.

26. Fred Moten, "Blackness and Poetry," sec. 2, par. 1.

27. Harney and Moten, *The Undercommons*, 140.

28. Theodor W. Adorno, *Problems of Moral Philosophy*, trans. Rodney Livingston (Cambridge: Polity, 2001), 167.

29. It is a little surprising that the leaders of these movements, whose theoretical orientations appeared indebted to Adorno, were disappointed with what they saw as a lack of radicalism on Adorno's part (see the tenth chapter of Rudolf Siebert's *Manifesto of the Critical Theory of Society and Religion*, vol. 2 [Leiden: Brill, 2010], 425–72). Adorno's work is unswerving in its rejection of political activism. The lack of enthusiasm for an emergent revolutionary class, the priority he gave in his writing to consumption and the culture industry in which class interest is all but redundant, his criticism of Bertolt Brecht's and Jean-Paul Sartre's attempts at political-aesthetic intervention, and, of course, his ambivalence toward Walter Benjamin's ideas concerning the progressive potentiality of mass media technology all betray this skepticism. He held fast to the belief that even when the intention is quite the opposite, engaging in programmatic work can make too much light of the "political reality . . . which then reduces the political effect." Theodor W. Adorno, "Commitment," *Performing Arts Journal* 3, no. 2 (1978): 11. Adorno gives the example of Charlie Chaplin's *The Great Dictator*, which "loses all satirical force, and becomes obscene, when a Jewish girl can bash a line of storm troopers on the head with a pan without being torn to pieces" (10–11).

30. Adorno, *Moral Philosophy*, 168.

31. Fabian Freyenhagen, *Adorno's Practical Philosophy: Living Less Wrongly* (Cambridge: Cambridge University Press, 2013), 150.

32. My point here is risky in light of the history of the appropriation of black enjoyment. What I am attempting to get at is the ideal of black expression that is *given* (although, Moten might say, it is not theirs/ours to give), not taken or sold. I have in mind an attitude or way of being that tends toward this (from Adorno): "All relations which are not distorted, indeed perhaps what is reconciliatory in organic life itself, are gifts." Gifts upset the exchange principle, although, as with everything else, the idea of giving or receiving a gift has become corrupted. Adorno again: "Human beings have forgotten how to give gifts, while pretending that such action is second nature in the social infrastructure that demands reciprocal gestures to be performed on specific occasions throughout the year. Violations of the exchange-principle have something absurdly unusual and unbelievable about them." Adorno, *Minima Moralia*, 42, 43.

33. Theodor W. Adorno, *Negative Dialectics*, trans. E. B. Ashton (London: Routledge, 1973), 6.

34. Fred Moten, "The Subprime and the Beautiful," *African Identities* 11, no. 2 (2013): 243.

35. Ibid.

36. Adorno, *Minima Moralia*, 39 (emphasis mine).

37. Anatoly Liberman, "The Growth of the English Etymological Dictionary," in *Adventuring in Dictionaries: New Studies in the History of Lexicography*, ed. John Considine (Newcastle: Cambridge Scholars, 2010), 168. See also Anatoly Liberman, "Our Habitat: Dwelling," *OUPblog*, Jan. 14, 2015, https://blog.oup.com/2015/01/dwelling-word-origin-etymology.

38. Moten, "The Subprime and the Beautiful," 243.

39. See Chapter 2 for more on Armstrong as furtive assailant. The song lyrics are from the bridge of the Fats Waller tune (with lyrics by Andy Razaf) "(What Did I Do to Be So) Black and Blue."

40. Mackey, "Andoumboulouous Brush," in *Splay Anthem*, 6.

41. Mackey, *Whatsaid Serif*, 30.

42. Nathaniel Mackey, "Epic World," interview by Joseph Donahue, Poetry Foundation website, May 6, 2014, www.poetryfoundation.org/articles/70116/epic-world.

43. John Coltrane, *Ascension*, Impulse! AS-95, A-95, 2009 [1965], compact disc.

44. Nathaniel Mackey, *Nod House* (New York: New Directions, 2011), 27.

45. See Mackey, "Song of the Andoumboulou: 55," in *Splay Anthem*, 93.

46. Billie Holiday, "I Loves You, Porgy" (1948), on *The Complete Decca Recordings*, MCA Records GRP 26012, 1991, compact disc.

47. Mackey, "Song of the Andoumboulou: 55," 93.

48. Mackey, "Song of the Andoumboulou: 34," in *Whatsaid Serif*, 100. Also, from Moten (and Stefano Harney): "Never being on the right side of the Atlantic is an unsettled feeling, the feeling of a thing that unsettles with others. It's a feeling, if you ride with it, that produces a certain distance from the settled, from those who determine themselves in space and time, who locate themselves in a determined history. To have been shipped is to have been moved by others, with others. It is to feel at home with the homeless, at ease with the fugitive, at peace with the pursued, at rest with the ones who consent not to be one." Harney and Moten, *The Undercommons*, 97.

49. According to Vijay Iyer:

> While rehearsing the precipitously difficult piece in the studio, John Coltrane can be heard saying to his struggling colleagues, "I don't think I'm gonna improve this, you know . . . I ain't goin be sayin nothin, (I goin do) tryin just, makin the changes, *I ain't goin be tellin no story . . . Like . . . tellin them black stories*." Amidst the confounded mumbles of assent from his bandmates, one colleague rejoins, "Shoot. *Really, you make the changes, that'll tell 'em a story*." Surprised by this idea, Coltrane responds, "*You think the changes're the story*!" Overlapping him, a second bandmate riffs, "*(Right) . . . that'll change all the stories (up)*." His voice cracking with laughter, Coltrane admits, "*I don't want to tell no lies (on 'em)*." After a group laugh, the second colleague trails off in a sort of denouement: "(The) changes themselves is some kind of story (man I'm tellin you)." (Vijay Iyer, "Exploding the Narrative in Jazz Improvi-

sation," in *Uptown Conversation: The New Jazz Studies*, ed. Robert G. O'Meally, Brent Hayes Edwards, and Farah Jasmine Griffin [New York: Columbia University Press, 2004], 394; emphasis mine)

50. Freyenhagen, *Adorno's Practical Philosophy*, 150.

51. In art music the musical material being formed by the composer is imbued with a sociohistory. That is to say, the scales and progressions that structure a piece, its stylistic convention and expressive direction, all carry within them the tradition and traces of broader society. The composer, in his or her use of a pool of collective content, is, in the work, reforming the tradition and, in doing so, representing in that work a community of temporally disparate composers. Adorno asserts, for example, that "all music, even that which is the most individualistic stylistically, has an inalienable collective content: each single sound already says 'We.'" This brings him into conversation with Coltrane, who tells us that "the audience heard 'we' even if the singer said 'I.'" Theodor Adorno quoted in Max Paddison, *Adorno's Aesthetics of Music* (Cambridge: Cambridge University Press, 1993), 115; John Coltrane quoted in McClary, *Conventional Wisdom: The Content of Musical Form* (Berkeley: University of California Press, 2000), 47.

52. Theodor W. Adorno, *Introduction to the Sociology of Music*, trans. E. B. Ashton (New York: Continuum, 1988), 18.

53. Rose Rosengard Subotnik, *Deconstructive Variations: Music and Reason in Western Society* (Minneapolis: University of Minnesota Press, 1996), 161–62.

54. Although the score was, for Adorno, crucial for interpretation, he did not dismiss reproduction (whether by performance or recording). For instance, he writes that "reproduction [performance] is necessary; music requires it, not simply to escape muteness, but for the sake of its immanent concern—as an answer, so to speak, to the question that music as such appears to pose through its very existence: how can music become a language and, vice versa, how can the symbol become an image?" Theodor W. Adorno, *Towards a Theory of Musical Reproduction: Notes, a Draft, and Two Schemata*, trans. Wieland Hoban (Cambridge: Polity, 2006), 180. On his conflicted views of recorded music see Theodor W. Adorno, "The Form of the Phonograph Record," trans. Thomas Y. Levin, *October* 55 (1990): 56–61; Theodor W. Adorno, "The Curves of the Needle," trans. Thomas Y. Levin, *October* 55 (1990): 49–55; and Thomas Y. Levin, "For the Record: Adorno on Music in the Age of its Technological Reproducibility," *October* 55 (1990): 23–47.

55. Freyenhagen, *Adorno's Practical Philosophy*, 170.

56. Subotnik, *Deconstructive Variations*, 154.

57. Ibid., 159.

58. Ibid., 161.

59. Theodor W. Adorno, "On Popular Music," in *Essays on Music*, selected, with introduction, commentary, and notes, by Richard Leppert, trans. Susan H. Gillespie (Berkeley: University of California Press, 2002), 446.

60. Subotnik, *Deconstructive Variations*, 187.

61. Moten, "Blackness and Poetry," sec. 2, par. 1.

62. Harney and Moten, *The Undercommons*, 97.

63. Benjamin, "The Storyteller," 100. For more on Benjamin and storytelling see Chapter 4.

64. Even where storytellers are home or community based, their stories are likely drawn from and carry their audience away from that intramural setting.

65. Benjamin, "The Storyteller," 99.

66. Subotnik, *Deconstructive Variations*, 161.

67. James Gordon Finlayson, "Adorno on the Ethical and the Ineffable," *European Journal of Philosophy* 10, no. 1 (2002): 1–25.

68. Adorno, *Moral Philosophy*, 169–70.

69. This idea comes from Harney and Moten in *The Undercommons*. Bessie Smith, "Gimme a Pigfoot" / "Take Me for a Buggy Ride," OKeh 8949, 1933, Shellac 10″.

70. Bessie Smith, "Nobody Knows You When You're Down and Out," Parlophone R2481, 1933, Shellac 10″.

71. This closing paragraph is very much enabled by Harney and Moten's *The Undercommons*. I also want to acknowledge the influence of the Black Study Group (London). A version of this paragraph was recorded for a segment called "Notes on Music and Money" for Paul Rekret's Resonance FM program, *Beholder Halfway*.

CHAPTER 4

1. Ornette Coleman, "Beauty Is a Rare Thing," on *This Is Our Music*, Ornette Coleman (alto), Don Cherry (trumpet), Charlie Haden (double bass), and Ed Blackwell (drums), Atlantic 1353, 2005 [1961], compact disc; Billie Holiday with Ray Ellis and his orchestra, "I'm a Fool to Want You," on *Lady in Satin*, Columbia/Legacy 88697 492002, 2009 [1958], compact disc. The two recordings were initially released a mere three years apart, but stylistically, Holiday and Coleman can be seen to inhabit markedly different eras. *Money Jungle*, a trio album recorded in 1962 featuring Duke Ellington, Charlie Mingus, and Max Roach is an example of a successful, if at times uneasy, alliance among musicians from different musical eras.

2. Fred Moten, *In the Break: The Aesthetics of the Black Radical Tradition* (Minneapolis: University of Minnesota Press, 2003), 107. Holiday is backed by an orchestra arrangement written by Ray Ellis. Interestingly, Charlie Parker's and Clifford Brown's experimentation with strings are similarly unsettling.

3. Andrew Benjamin, "Event, Time, Repetition," *Columbia Documents of Architecture and Theory* 4 (1999): 140.

4. Walter Benjamin, "The Storyteller: Reflections on the Works of Nikolai Leskov," in *Illuminations: Essays and Reflections* (London: Fontana, 1992). See Andrew Benjamin, *Present Hope: Philosophy, Architecture, Judaism* (London: Routledge, 1997), 55; and Rajeev S. Patke, "Benjamin on Art and Reproducibility: The Case of Music," in *Walter Benjamin and Art*, ed. Andrew Benjamin (London: Continuum, 2005), 196.

5. William Francis Allen quoted in Shane White and Graham J. White, *The Sounds of Slavery: Discovering African American History Through Songs, Sermons, and Speech* (Boston: Beacon, 2005), 64.

6. "Body and Soul" (written by Johnny Green in 1930 with lyrics by Edward Hey-

man, Robert Sour, and Frank Eyton) is undoubtedly one of the most performed jazz standards. It holds an iconic status, with several important versions recorded by vocalists. But its significance is, perhaps, better explained by Coleman Hawkins's 1939 recording, which appears to hold the tradition's past and future in balance. See discography for locations of the interpretation I allude to.

7. For a detailed discussion on storytelling in jazz see my essay "Storytelling in Jazz Work as Retrospective Collaboration." *Journal of the Society for American Music* 11, no. 1 (2017): 70–92.

8. Brian Harker, *Louis Armstrong's Hot Five and Hot Seven Recordings* (New York: Oxford University Press, 2011), 41.

9. Gunther Schuller, *The Swing Era: The Development of Jazz, 1930–1945* (New York: Oxford University Press, 1991), 548.

10. Scott DeVeaux, *The Birth of Bebop: A Social and Musical History* (Berkeley: University of California Press, 1997), 97–98.

11. Paul Berliner, *Thinking in Jazz: The Infinite Art of Improvisation* (Chicago: University of Chicago Press, 1994), 202.

12. Buck Clayton quoted in Douglas Henry Daniels, "Lester Young: Master of Jive," *American Music* 3, no. 3 (1985): 318.

13. There is a plethora of accounts, including James Snead's "On Repetition in Black Culture," *Black American Literature Forum* 15, no. 4 (1981): 146–54; various texts from Amiri Baraka; and Monson's work, particularly "Riffs, Repetition, and Theories of Globalization," *Ethnomusicology* 43, no. 1 (1999): 31–65. Norman Weinstein's underappreciated essay on the Art Ensemble of Chicago is also important; see Norman Weinstein, "Steps Toward an Integrative Comprehension of the Art Ensemble of Chicago's Music," *Lenox Avenue: A Journal of Interarts Inquiry* 3 (1997): 5–11.

14. I have in mind here both Adorno's "Schubert (1928)" and James Snead's 1981 mischievous corroboration of Hegel's thesis regarding the Sub-Saharan African remaining outside history. Snead writes, provocatively, "Hegel was almost entirely correct in his reading of black culture. . . . The African, first, overturns all European categories of logic. Secondly, he has no idea of history or progress. . . . Finally, he is 'immediate' and intimately tied to nature with all its cyclical, non-progressive data. Having no self-consciousness, he is 'immediate'—i.e., *always there*—in any given moment. Here we can see that, being there, the African is also *always already there*, or perhaps *always there before*, whereas the European is *headed there* or, better, *not yet there*." Snead, "On Repetition in Black Culture," 148.

15. Benjamin, "The Storyteller," 92.

16. Edward M. Pavlić, *Crossroads Modernism: Descent and Emergence in African-American Literary Culture* (Minneapolis: University of Minnesota Press, 2002), 24. This is a facet of traditional forms retained in modern European music, although with important distinctions. Whereas the work of classical pieces is most often considered to be within the score (various performers being interpreters who bring out new aspects of the piece), the work of the story is thought to be within its performance. The hub of creativity—as in, making the work—of jazz is located in performance; conversely, in

European music the performer is most often charged with following the written intentions of the composer.

17. Martin T. Williams, *The Jazz Tradition* (New York: Oxford University Press, 1993); Gunther Schuller, "Sonny Rollins and the Challenge of Thematic Improvisation," *Jazz Review* 1, no. 1 (1958): 6–11. For a discussion taking in the broader field of (ethno) musicology, see Georgina Born, "On Musical Mediation: Ontology, Technology and Creativity," *Twentieth-Century Music* 2, no. 7 (2005): 7–36. Drawing from Alfred Gell's 1998 anthropological study *Art and Agency*, a notion of art objects as fluid assemblages is presented. Works are structured by relations among creators, audience, and works, exhibiting an "extended mind" in which these various actors are linked across space and time.

18. Mimesis as used by Benjamin and Adorno is notoriously difficult to understand, and its interpretation by subsequent scholars tends only to add to the confusion. That said, Bed Paudyal's 2009 identification of five senses of mimesis used by Adorno is helpful for orientation. See Bed Paudyal, "Mimesis in Adorno's Aesthetic Theory," *Journal of Philosophy* 4, no. 8 (2009): 1–10. In *Adorno's Aesthetics of Music* (Cambridge: Cambridge University Press, 1993) Max Paddison appears to lean toward the more anthropological connotations, presenting it as a version of mimicry, an adapting to the hostile environment as a form of protection. (There is an interesting discussion to be had regarding the use of mimicry in black expression—for example, minstrelsy and certain types of signifying.) However, in a more considered recent essay, "Mimesis and the Aesthetics of Musical Expression," Paddison comes much closer to the reading presented here. See Max Paddison, "Mimesis and the Aesthetics of Musical Expression," *Music Analysis* 29, nos. 1–3 (2010): 126–48, esp. 134–35. See also Gary Peters, *The Philosophy of Improvisation* (Chicago: University of Chicago Press, 2009) for what is by far the most engaged recent account of mimesis in improvised music. Peters perhaps overstates (and confuses) the case when he writes, "Adorno's aesthetic theory promotes a mimeticism that . . . has nothing whatever to do with imitating or copying that which is already given" (86); nevertheless, the processual dimensions and ethical connotations of the concept are effectively emphasized.

19. This idea is enabled by Andrew Benjamin's incisive remarks on intimacy:

> To be fascinated by something necessitates a distance. If one gets too close, one is no longer fascinated. To maintain curiosity also necessitates maintaining a certain distance.
>
> What interests me about all of these words (love, curiosity, fascination) is the way in which they hold a certain fragility. They all imply distance as a central notion, which does not mean distance in the sense of not getting close, but distance in the sense of abandoning oneself, whereby one abandons the idea of mastering the situation. To love someone is to abandon one's mastery of time as much as the mastery of oneself. One cannot make another person love. One cannot stop someone from loving. Love is in fact the ultimate form of abandoning desire for mastery. (Andrew Benjamin, "Spacing as an Art," in *Territorial Investigations*, ed. Annette W. Balkema and Henk Slager [Amsterdam: Rodopi, 1999], 17)

20. Albrecht Wellmer quoted in Paddison, "Mimesis and the Aesthetics of Musical Expression," 139.

21. This calls to mind Adorno's idea concerning a performance of a modern European work always falling short, as it will fail to include all the possible connotations contained in the work. Does Coltrane's interpretation of "Body and Soul" create—that is, add to—the original work? Adorno would argue that his work was already contained in the idea of the piece.

22. See discography for details. The Dexter Gordon version I am thinking of is the 1978 live recording, featuring George Cables (piano), Rufus Reid (bass), and Eddie Gladden (drums). For analysis see Cynthia Folio and Alexander Brinkman, "Dexter Gordon's Ultimate 'Body and Soul,'" in *Five Perspectives on "Body and Soul,"* ed. Claudia Emmenegger and Oliver Senn (Zurich: Lucerne School of Music, 2011), 45–60, esp. 45–46. For an encyclopedic consideration of the standard see José Antonio Bowen, "Who Plays the Tune in 'Body and Soul'? A Performance History Using Recorded Sources," *Journal of the Society for American Music* 9, no. 3 (2015): 259–92.

23. Charles Mingus (with Eric Dolphy), "Sophisticated Lady," on *Cornell 1964*, Blue Note 0946 3 92210 2 8, 2007 [1964], compact disc.

24. Eric Dolphy, when on bass clarinet, tends to use a similar mixture of his idiosyncratic bebop and vocal articulation. It is interesting to contrast this technique with what he uses on flute, which, while singerly, tends to use a more limited, vocal-like expressive palate.

25. Jessica Williams, referring to Thelonious Monk's technique. See Jessica Williams, "Thelonious Sphere Monk," Jessica Williams—Currents (personal website, March 1998), www.jessicawilliams.com/currents/monk.html.

26. Vijay Iyer, "Exploding the Narrative in Jazz Improvisation," in *Uptown Conversation: The New Jazz Studies*, ed. Robert G. O'Meally, Brent Hayes Edwards, and Farah Jasmine Griffin (New York: Columbia University Press, 2004), 402.

27. *Technique* is a tricky word to use here, as in a sense technique is the key; however, it is the "homemade" variety that is of importance. Technical ability should also include the ways of effectively contributing while playing to (and with) one's strengths and limitations.

28. Benjamin, "The Storyteller," 91.

29. Ibid., 91, 90. Listening to jazz, particularly for musicians and other contributors, seems to require both the absorption Benjamin prescribes *and* what Adorno describes as "structural listening."

30. Ibid., 91.

31. John Robert Brown, *A Concise History of Jazz* (Pacific, MO: Mel Bay, 2010), 100.

32. Eunmi Shim, *Lennie Tristano: His Life in Music* (Ann Arbor: University of Michigan Press, 2007), 135.

33. There is interesting work to be done exploring Benjamin's storytelling listener alongside Adorno's structural and regressive listener. Keeping in mind the retrospective from which Benjamin brings us the portrait of the storyteller, his work provides an important alternative to Adorno's stratification of listening types.

34. Susan McClary, *Conventional Wisdom: The Content of Musical Form* (Berke-

ley: University of California Press, 2000), 34. McClary argues that the blues and its lineage are of central importance, and should have a prominent place, in "any account of twentieth-century Western music." She also writes, "When LeRoi Jones [Amiri Baraka] published his powerful book *Blues People* in 1963, his title referred to the African American musicians who fashioned the blues out of their particular historical conditions and experience. Yet a music scholar of a future time might well look back on the musical landscape of the 1900s and label us all 'blues people': those who inhabited a period dominated by blues and its countless progeny" (32–33).

35. Alan Lomax quoted in Robert Switzer, "Signifying the Blues," *Alif: Journal of Comparative Poetics* 21 (2001): 40.

36. Eddie "Son" House, "Dry Spell Blues Part I / Dry Spell Blues Part II," Paramount 12990, 1930, Shellac 10″.

37. Benjamin, "The Storyteller," 84.

38. Theodor W. Adorno, *Aesthetic Theory*, trans. Robert Hullot-Kentor (Minneapolis: University of Minnesota Press, 1997), 40.

39. Frederick Douglass, *Narrative of the Life of Frederick Douglass: An American Slave* (New York: Simon and Schuster, 2004), 35.

40. Ibid., 34.

41. Ibid., 33–34.

42. Nathaniel Mackey puts it this way: "One of the reasons the music so often goes over into nonspeech—moaning, humming, shouts, nonsense lyrics, scat—is to say, among other things, that the realm of conventionally articulate speech is not sufficient for saying what needs to be said." Nathaniel Mackey, "Cante moro," in *Paracritical Hinge: Essays, Talks, Notes, Interviews* (Madison: University of Wisconsin Press, 2005), 193.

These sounds at times slide into components more closely associated with formal music practice. Listen to how Holiday bends the word *thrill* in the opening phrase of the 1949 recording of "You're My Thrill" and how Mingus's bass seems to sigh through a cascading pizzicato figure at the opening of "Orange Was the Color of Her Dress, Then Blue Silk." It sounds as though the exhalation has been aurally pixelated. The sigh has been given certain analytic possibilities hitherto not ascribed to it. Mingus uses a very similar figure in "Fleurette Africaine" on the album *Money Jungle*. Drummer Max Roach makes comparable use of "embodied" figure in a four-note, quietly irregular, drum pattern, suggesting something between heartbeat and sigh.

43. Here I am influenced by M. NourbeSe Philip's storytelling in *Zong!*, particularly the turn, in her poetry, toward engaging the reader to feel (with) her and Setaey Adamu Boateng the imagined lost slave from whom Philip heard the story. It may be that the story that cannot be told but must be can be *felt* more keenly than it can be known (within our conventional understanding of what it is to know something). See M. NourbeSe Philip, *Zong!* (Middletown, CT: Wesleyan University Press, 2008).

44. Switzer, "Signifying the Blues," 54. Switzer is drawing from unpublished research on early twentieth-century delta blues by the late Tom Lamont.

45. Sam Chatmon quoted in Switzer, "Signifying the Blues," 54.

46. Billie Holiday featuring the Gordon Jenkins Orchestra, "You're My Thrill," in

The Complete Decca Recordings, MCA Records GRP 26012, 1991, compact disc; Charles Mingus Sextet, featuring Eric Dolphy, "Orange Was the Color of Her Dress, Then Blue Silk," on *Cornell 1964*, Blue Note 0946 3 92210 2 8, 2007 [1964], compact disc; Duke Ellington, Charles Mingus, and Max Roach, "Fleurette Africaine," on *Money Jungle*, Blue Note 7243 5 38227 2 9, 2002 [1963], compact disc.

47. Theodor Adorno, *Aesthetic Theory*, trans. Christian Lenhardt (London: Routledge, 1984), 59.

48. Saidiya Hartman, *Scenes of Subjection: Terror, Slavery, and Self-Making in Nineteenth-Century America* (New York: Oxford University Press, 1997), 33.

49. Ibid., 43.

50. Ibid., 4.

51. Ibid., 35.

52. Theodor Adorno, "The Perennial Fashion—Jazz," in *The Adorno Reader*, ed. Brian O'Connor (Oxford: Blackwell, 2000), 269.

53. See Édouard Glissant, *Poetics of Relation* (Ann Arbor: University of Michigan Press, 1997).

54. Saidiya Hartman, "The Position of the Unthought," interview by Frank B. Wilderson III, *Qui Parle* 13, no. 2 (2003): 185.

55. Theodor Adorno, "Trying to Understand *Endgame*," in *Can One Live After Auschwitz? A Philosophical Reader*, ed. Rolf Tiedemann (Stanford, CA: Stanford University Press, 2003), 261.

56. Andrew Bowie, *Music, Philosophy, and Modernity* (Cambridge: Cambridge University Press, 2007), 11. Bowie's work has been on European art music, but the philosopher, who is also a jazz saxophonist, has declared his interest: "Although the experience of jazz improvisation has revealed itself in the course of writing to be more fundamental to what I have to say than I originally realised, I do not give a specific account of it, preferring to take up those aspects of philosophy concerned with music which relate to the intuitions I have gained from playing jazz" (14).

57. Fred Moten and Charles Henry Rowell, " 'Words Don't Go There': An Interview with Fred Moten," *Callaloo* 27, no. 4 (2004): 962.

58. See Brent Hayes Edwards's recently published *Epistrophies: Jazz and the Literary Imagination* for further evidence of such (Cambridge: Harvard University Press, 2017). Edwards's excellent text is a very welcome contribution to what I have here termed empathetic jazz scholarship. Also see, Meta DuEwa Jones's insightful *The Muse is Music: Jazz Poetry from the Harlem Renaissance to Spoken Word* (Champaign: University of Illinois Press, 2011).

59. Iyer, "Exploding the Narrative," 395.

60. See, e.g., his serial novel *From a Broken Bottle Traces of Perfume Still Emanate* and his serial poems "Mu" and "Song of the Andoumboulou" spread across several collections including *Splay Anthem* (New York: New Directions, 2006) and *Blue Fasa* (New York: New Directions, 2015).

61. Mackey, *From a Broken Bottle*, 51. See Chapter 3 for more on black unworlding or worldlessness.

62. Mackey, *From a Broken Bottle*, 50. See also Adorno, "The Perennial Fashion—Jazz," 276–78. For critique see Krin Gabbard, "Signifyin(g) the Phallus: *Mo' Better Blues* and Representations of the Jazz Trumpet," in *Representing Jazz*, ed. Krin Gabbard (Durham, NC: Duke University Press, 1995), 104.

63. "Triptych," on *We Insist! Max Roach's Freedom Now Suite* (1960); Mingus's wails on "Haitian Fight Song" (1957); Scott Saul, *Freedom Is, Freedom Ain't: Jazz and the Making of the Sixties* (Cambridge, MA: Harvard University Press, 2003), 2.

64. Abbey Lincoln and Max Roach, "Triptych," on *We Insist! Max Roach's Freedom Now Suite*, Candid CCD 79002, 1990 [1960], compact disc.

65. Weinstein, "Steps Toward an Integrative Comprehension," 5.

66. Robert Walser, "Out of Notes: Signification, Interpretation, and the Problem of Miles Davis," in *Jazz Among the Discourses*, ed. Krin Gabbard (Durham, NC: Duke University Press, 1995), 169. As Walser points out, this is not a situation confined to jazz. Does traditional analysis usefully engage with the diversity and depth of the modern European tradition? Similarly, Carolyn Abbate, in "Music—Drastic or Gnostic?" *Critical Inquiry* 30, no. 3 (2004), following Vladimir Jankélévitch, points out the limitations of the work-as-composition of the tradition. She suggests that "musical sounds are made by labor. And it is in the irreversible experience of playing, singing, or listening that any meanings summoned by music come into being. Retreating to the work displaces that experience, and dissecting the work's technical features or saying what it represents reflects the wish not to be transported by the state that the performance has engendered in us" (505–6).

67. John Coltrane quoted in Don DeMichael, "John Coltrane and Eric Dolphy Answer the Critics," *Downbeat*, Apr. 12, 1962, 20–23.

68. Moten and Rowell, "Words Don't Go There," 956. See also Moten's collection of poems, *B Jenkins* (Durham, NC: Duke University Press, 2009).

69. Bowie, *Music, Philosophy and Modernity*, 11–12.

POSTSCRIPT

1. I have settled on the word *record* to refer to any audio documentation of jazz music. *Record* is a placeholder for compact disc, tape, mp3, and any other such audio format.

2. Notwithstanding Wynton Marsalis's evocative "reconstruction" of Bolden over the years. Listen, for example, to "The Legend of Buddy Bolden," on *Citi Movement (Griot New York)*, Columbia, COL 473055 2, 1993, compact disc.

3. Original Dixieland Jass Band, "Dixieland Jass Band One Step / Livery Stable Blues," Victor 18255, 1917, Shellac 10″. Buddy Bolden had been confined to the East Louisiana State Hospital for ten years by the time the Original Dixieland Jass Band cut "Livery Stable Blues."

4. Nonrecorded jazz, regardless of when it is performed, is perhaps better termed ante-/antihistory. We have no record of this supposedly lost-in-the-moment work, but the multitude of instances of nonrecorded "play" is what (most) jazz recording is a response to. The two arenas stand in apposition.

5. Since the advent of digital home recording the constraints of format have become less significant, although the costs involved in use of a recording studio has meant that for many musicians, time limitations have migrated from format over to studio time/cost.

6. Commercial practice and rehearsal space might also elicit a similar anxiety fueled by "getting one's money's worth."

7. Walter Benjamin, "The Work of Art in the Age of Mechanical Reproduction," in *Illuminations: Essays and Reflections* (London: Fontana, 1992), 215.

8. See Michael Heller's excellent discussion of the qualitative differences between recordings of rehearsals and those of studio projects. Michael Heller, *Loft Jazz* (Oakland: University of California Press, 2016), 155–60.

9. Theodor W. Adorno, "On Jazz," trans. Jamie Owen Daniel, *Discourse* 12, no. 1 (1989–90): 47.

10. Charles Mingus, "Fables of Faubus," on *Mingus Ah Um*, Columbia 88697127572, 2007 [1959], compact disc.

11. Salim Washington, "'All the Things You Could Be by Now': *Charles Mingus Presents Charles Mingus* and the Limits of Avant-Garde Jazz," in *Uptown Conversation: The New Jazz Studies*, ed. Robert G. O'Meally, Brent Hayes Edwards, and Farah Jasmine Griffin (New York: Columbia University Press, 2004), 39. Charles Mingus, "Fables of Faubus," on *Charles Mingus Presents Charles Mingus*, Candid CCD 79005, 2000 [1960], compact disc.

12. Scott Saul, *Freedom Is, Freedom Ain't: Jazz and the Making of the Sixties* (Cambridge, MA: Harvard University Press, 2003), 204.

13. Charles Mingus Sextet with Eric Dolphy, "Fables of Faubus," on *Cornell 1964*, Blue Note 0946 3 92210 2 8, 2007 [1964], compact disc.

14. I am bracketing the fact that live performance is often also time-constrained, although I believe that the qualitative difference stands.

15. Adorno quoted in David Jenemann, *Adorno in America* (Minneapolis: University of Minnesota Press, 2007), 114.

16. Fabian Freyenhagen, *Adorno's Practical Philosophy: Living Less Wrongly* (Cambridge: Cambridge University Press, 2013), 150.

17. Stephen Henderson, *Understanding the New Black Poetry: Black Speech and Black Music as Poetic References* (New York: Morrow, 1973), 44.

BIBLIOGRAPHY

"AACM Panel Discussion." Center for Computer Research in Music and Acoustics (CCRMA), Stanford University, May 12, 2014. YouTube video. Posted by "ccrmalite1," July 3, 2014. www.youtube.com/watch?v=HuT8r8D0w3Q.

Abbate, Carolyn. "Music—Drastic or Gnostic?" *Critical Inquiry* 30, no. 3 (2004): 505–36.

Aboulafia, Mitchell. "W. E. B. Du Bois: Double Consciousness, Jamesian Sympathy, and the Critical Turn." In *The Oxford Handbook of American Philosophy*, edited by Cheryl Misak, 169–84. Oxford: Oxford University Press, 2008.

Adorno, Theodor W. *Aesthetic Theory*. Translated by Christian Lenhardt. London: Routledge, 1984.

———. *Aesthetic Theory*. Translated by Robert Hullot-Kentor. Minneapolis: University of Minnesota Press, 1997.

———. "Commitment." *Performing Arts Journal* 3, no. 2 (1978): 3–11.

———. *Critical Models: Interventions and Catchwords*. Translated by Henry W. Pickford. New York: Columbia University Press, 2005.

———. *The Culture Industry: Selected Essays on Mass Culture*. Edited by J. M. Bernstein. London: Routledge, 2001.

———. "Culture Industry Reconsidered." Translated by Anson G. Rabinbach. *New German Critique*, no. 6 (Fall 1975): 12–19.

———. "The Curves of the Needle." Translated by Thomas Y. Levin. *October* 55 (1990): 49–55.

———. *Essays on Music*. Selected, with introduction, commentary, and notes, by Richard Leppert. New translations by Susan H. Gillespie. Berkeley: University of California Press, 2002.

———. "The Form of the Phonograph Record." Translated by Thomas Y. Levin. *October* 55 (1990): 56–61.

———. "Free Time." In *Critical Models*, 167–76.

———. "Freudian Theory and the Pattern of Fascist Propaganda." In *The Culture Industry*, 132–57.

———. *Introduction to the Sociology of Music*. New York: Continuum, 1988.

———. *Minima Moralia: Reflections on a Damaged Life*. Translated by E. F. N. Jephcott. London: Verso, 2005.

———. *Negative Dialectics*. Translated by E. B. Ashton. London: Routledge, 1973.

———. "On Jazz." Translated by Jamie Owen Daniel, *Discourse* 12, no. 1 (1989–90): 45–69.

———. "On Popular Music." In *Essays on Music*, 437–69.

———. "On the Fetish-Character in Music and the Regression of Listening." In *Essays on Music*, 288–317.

———. "On the Social Situation of Music." In *Essays on Music*, 391–436.

———. "The Perennial Fashion—Jazz." In *The Adorno Reader*, edited by Brian O'Connor, 267–79. Oxford: Blackwell, 2000.

———. *Philosophy of Modern Music*. London: A&C Black, 2003.

———. *Problems of Moral Philosophy*. Translated by Rodney Livingston. Cambridge: Polity, 2001.

———. "Schubert (1928)." Translated by Jonathan Dunsby and Beate Perrey. *19th Century Music* 29, no. 1 (2005): 3–14.

———. "On Subject and Object." In *Critical Models*, 245–58.

———. *Towards a Theory of Musical Reproduction: Notes, a Draft, and Two Schemata*. Translated by Weiland Hoban. Cambridge: Polity, 2006.

———. "Trying to Understand *Endgame*." Translated by Shierry Weber Nicholsen. In *Can One Live After Auschwitz? A Philosophical Reader*, edited by Rolf Tiedemann, 259–94. Stanford, CA: Stanford University Press, 2003.

Adorno, Theodor W., Walter Benjamin, Ernst Bloch, Bertolt Brecht, and Georg Lukács. *Aesthetics and Politics*. London: Verso, 2010.

Adorno, Theodor W., and Joachim-Ernst Berendt. "Pro and Contra Jazz." *German History in Documents and Images* 8 (1953): http://germanhistorydocs.ghi-dc.org/pdf/eng/Vol.8_Chap.27_Doc.05_ENGL.pdf.

Adorno, Theodor, and Max Horkheimer. *Towards a New Manifesto*. London: Verso, 2011.

Anderson, Iain. *This Is Our Music: Free Jazz, the Sixties, and American Culture*. Philadelphia: University of Pennsylvania Press, 2007.

Aptheker, Herbert. Introduction to *W. E. B. Du Bois: Against Racism: Unpublished Essays, Papers, Addresses, 1887–1961*. Edited by Herbert Aptheker, xi–xiii. Amherst: University of Massachusetts Press, 1988.

Austerlitz, Paul. *Jazz Consciousness: Music, Race, and Humanity*. Middletown, CT: Wesleyan University Press, 2005.

Baraka, Amiri. *Black Music: Essays by LeRoi Jones (Amiri Baraka)*. New York: Akashic, 2010.

———. *Blues People: Negro Music in White America*. New York: Perennial, 2002.

———. *Digging: The Afro-American Soul of American Classical Music*. Berkeley: University of California Press, 2009.

———. *Dutchman*. In *The LeRoi Jones/Amiri Baraka Reader*, 76–99.

———. *The LeRoi Jones/Amiri Baraka Reader*. Edited by William J. Harris. New York: Thunder's Mouth, 1999.

Benjamin, Andrew. "Event, Time, Repetition." *Columbia Documents of Architecture and Theory* 4 (1999): 139–47.

———. *Present Hope: Philosophy, Architecture, Judaism*. London: Routledge, 1997.

———. "Spacing as an Art." In *Territorial Investigations*, edited by Annette W. Balkema and Henk Slager, 13–22. Amsterdam, The Netherlands: Rodopi, 1999.

Benjamin, Walter. *Illuminations: Essays and Reflections*. London: Fontana, 1992.

———. *Selected Writings: 1913–1926*. Cambridge, MA: Harvard University Press, 1996.

———. "The Storyteller: Reflections on the Works of Nikolai Leskov." In *Illuminations*, 81–107.

———. "The Work of Art in the Age of Mechanical Reproduction." In *Illuminations*, 211–44.

Berliner, Paul. *Thinking in Jazz: The Infinite Art of Improvisation*. Chicago: University of Chicago Press, 1994.

Block, Steven. "'Bemsha Swing': The Transformation of a Bebop Classic to Free Jazz." *Music Theory Spectrum* 19, no. 2 (1997): 206–31.

Borgo, David. "The Play of Meaning and the Meaning of Play in Jazz." *Journal of Consciousness Studies* 11, no. 3/4 (2004): 174–90.

———. *Sync or Swarm: Improvising Music in a Complex Age*. New York: Continuum, 2005.

Borgo, David, and Jeff Kaiser. "Configurin(g) KaiBorg: Ideology, Identity and Agency." *Electro-Acoustic Improvised Music Beyond the Centres: Musical Avant-Gardes Since 1950*, conference proceedings, 2010, 1–8.

Born, Georgina. "On Musical Mediation: Ontology, Technology and Creativity." *Twentieth-Century Music* 2, no. 1 (2005): 7–36.

Bowen, José Antonio. "Who Plays the Tune in 'Body and Soul'? A Performance History Using Recorded Sources." *Journal of the Society for American Music* 9, no. 3 (2015): 259–92.

Bowie, Andrew. *Music, Philosophy, and Modernity*. Cambridge: Cambridge University Press, 2007.

Brown, John Robert. *A Concise History of Jazz*. Pacific, MO: Mel Bay, 2010.

Brown, Lee. "Adorno's Critique of Popular Culture: The Case of Jazz Music." *Journal of Aesthetic Education* 21, no. 1 (1992): 17–31.

———. Postmodernist Jazz Theory." *Journal of Aesthetic Education* 57, no. 2 (1999): 235–46.

Brown, Leonard L. "In His Own Words: Coltrane's Responses to Critics." In *John Coltrane and Black America's Quest*, 11–31.

———, ed. *John Coltrane and Black America's Quest for Freedom: Spirituality and the Music*. New York: Oxford University Press, 2010.

Buck-Morss, Susan. *The Origin of Negative Dialectics: Theodor W. Adorno, Walter Benjamin, and the Frankfurt Institute*. New York: Free Press, 1977.

Buhler, James. “Frankfurt School Blues: Rethinking Adorno's Critique of Jazz.” In *Apparitions: New Perspectives on Adorno and Twentieth-Century Music*, edited by Berthold Hoeckner, 103–30. New York: Routledge, 2006.

Burger, Peter. *Theory of the Avant-Garde*. Manchester: Manchester University Press, 1984.

Césaire, Aimé. *Discourse on Colonialism*. New York: Monthly Review Press, 2000.

Chandler, Nahum D. “Of Exorbitance: The Problem of the Negro as a Problem for Thought.” *Criticism* 50, no. 3 (2008): 345–410.

———. “Of Horizon: An Introduction to ‘The Afro-American’ by W. E. B. Du Bois—circa 1894.” *Journal of Transnational American Studies* 2, no. 1 (2010): 1–41.

———. “Originary Displacement.” *boundary 2* 27, no. 3 (2000): 249–86.

———. *X—The Problem of the Negro as a Problem for Thought*. New York: Fordham University Press, 2014.

Coltrane, John. “Interview with John Coltrane by Carl-Eric Lindgren.” Stockholm, March 21, 1960. YouTube video. Posted March 19, 2015. www.youtube.com/watch?v=TdBQbu5ADhw.

Comay, Rebecca. “Adorno's Siren Song.” *New German Critique*, no. 81 (Autumn 2000): 21–48.

Cook, Deborah. *The Culture Industry Revisited: Theodor W. Adorno on Mass Culture*. Lanham, MD: Rowman and Littlefield, 1996.

Daniel, Jamie Owen. “Achieving Subjectlessness: Reassessing the Politics of Adorno's Subject of Modernity.” *Cultural Logic: An Electronic Journal of Marxist Theory and Practice* 3, no. 1 (1999): http://clogic.eserver.org/3-1&2/daniel.html.

———. “Introduction to Theodor W. Adorno's ‘On Jazz.’ ” *Discourse* 12, no. 1 (1989–90): 39–44.

Daniels, Douglas Henry. “Lester Young: Master of Jive.” *American Music* 3, no. 3 (1985): 313–28.

Davis, Angela. “Reflections on the Black Woman's Role in the Community of Slaves.” In *Words of Fire: An Anthology of African-American Feminist Thought*, edited by Beverly Guy-Sheftall, 200–218. New York: New Press, 1995.

DeVeaux, Scott. *The Birth of Bebop: A Social and Musical History*. Berkeley: University of California Press, 1997.

———. “Constructing the Jazz Tradition: Jazz Historiography.” *Black American Literature* 25, no. 3 (1991): 525–60.

DeMichael, Don. “John Coltrane and Eric Dolphy Answer the Critics.” *Downbeat*, Apr. 12, 1962, 20–23.

Dewey, John. “The Live Creature and ‘Ethereal Things.’ ” In *The Later Works of John Dewey, 1925–1953*, edited by Jo Ann Boydston. Volume 10: 1934, *Art as Experience*, 26–41. Carbondale: Southern Illinois University Press, 1987.

Dorr-Dorynek, Diane. “Mingus . . . ” In *The Jazz Word*, edited by Dom Cerulli, Burt Korall, and Mort L. Nasatir. New York: Ballantine, 1987.

Douglass, Frederick. *Narrative of the Life of Frederick Douglass: An American Slave*. New York: Simon and Schuster, 2004.

Du Bois, W. E. B. *Against Racism: Unpublished Essays, Papers, Addresses, 1887–1961*. Edited by Herbert Aptheker. Amherst: University of Massachusetts Press, 1988.

———. "Beyond the Veil in a Virginia Town (1897)." In *Against Racism*, 49–50.

———. *The Souls of Black Folk*. 1903. New York: Dover, 1994.

Du Bois, W. E. B., and Isabel Eaton. *The Philadelphia Negro: A Social Study*. New York: Schocken, 1967.

Dunaway, Wilma. *The African-American Family in Slavery and Emancipation*. Cambridge: Cambridge University Press, 2003.

Dunkel, Mario. *Aesthetics of Resistance: Charles Mingus and the Civil Rights Movement*. Zurich: Lit Verlag, 2012.

Edwards, Brent Hayes. *Epistrophies: Jazz and the Literary Imagination*. Cambridge, MA: Harvard University Press, 2017.

Ellison, Ralph. "The Charlie Christian Story." In *Shadow and Act*, 233–40.

———. *Invisible Man*. London: Penguin, 2001.

———. "The Seer and the Seen." In *Shadow and Act*, 3–183.

———. *Shadow and Act*. New York: Vintage International, 1995.

Fanon, Frantz. *Black Skin, White Masks*. London: Pluto, 2008.

Feinstein, Sasha, and Yusef Komunyakaa, eds. *The Jazz Poetry Anthology*. Bloomington: Indiana University Press, 1991.

Finlayson, James Gordon. "Adorno on the Ethical and the Ineffable." *European Journal of Philosophy* 10, no. 1 (2002): 1–25.

Folio, Cynthia, and Alexander Brinkman. "Dexter Gordon's Ultimate 'Body and Soul.'" In *Five Perspectives on "Body and Soul,"* edited by Claudia Emmenegger and Oliver Senn, 45–60. Zurich: Lucerne School of Music, 2011.

Fox, Robert. "Coming of Age with the Blues." *Massachusetts Review* 37, no. 4 (1996): 621–35.

Freyenhagen, Fabian. *Adorno's Practical Philosophy: Living Less Wrongly*. Cambridge: Cambridge University Press, 2013.

Gabbard, Krin, ed. *Jazz Among the Discourses*. Durham, NC: Duke University Press, 1995.

———. "Signifyin(g) the Phallus: *Mo' Better Blues* and Representations of Jazz Trumpet." In *Representing Jazz*, edited by Krin Gabbard, 104–30. Durham, NC: Duke University Press, 1995.

Gates, Henry Louis. *The Signifying Monkey: A Theory of Afro-American Literary Criticism*. New York: Oxford University Press, 1988.

Genovese, Eugene. *Roll, Jordan, Roll: The World the Slaves Made*. New York: Pantheon, 1974.

Giddins, Gary. *Visions of Jazz: The First Century*. Oxford: Oxford University Press, 1998.

Gilroy, Paul. *The Black Atlantic: Modernity and Double Consciousness*. Cambridge, MA: Harvard University Press, 1993.

Gioia, Ted. "Jazz and the Primitivist Myth." *Musical Quarterly* 73, no. 1 (1989): 130–43.

Glissant, Édouard. *Poetics of Relation*. Ann Arbor: University of Michigan Press, 1997.

Goffin, Robert. "The Best Negro Jazz Orchestras." In *Beckett in Black and Red: The*

Translations for Nancy Cunard's "Negro" (1934), edited by Alan Warren Friedman, 4–9. Lexington: University Press of Kentucky, 2000.

———. *Horn of Plenty: The Story of Louis Armstrong*. New York: Da Capo, 1977.

———. *Jazz: From the Congo to the Metropolitan*. Translated by Walter Schaap and Leonard Feather. 1944. Cambridge, MA: De Capo, 1975.

Gooding-Williams, Robert. *In the Shadow of Du Bois: Afro-Modern Political Thought in America*. Cambridge, MA: Harvard University Press, 2010.

Gordon, Lewis R. *Her Majesty's Other Children: Sketches of Racism from a Neocolonial Age*. Lanham, MD: Rowman and Littlefield, 1997.

Gracyk, Theodore. "Adorno, Jazz, and the Aesthetics of Popular Music." *Musical Quarterly* 76, no. 4 (1992): 526–42.

Gridley, Mark. "Misconceptions of Linking Free Jazz with the Civil Rights Movement." *College Music Symposium* 47 (2007): 139–55.

———. "Perception of Emotion in Jazz Improvisation." *Advances in Psychology Research* 62 (Jan. 2010): 163–84.

Griffith, Jennifer. "Mingus in the Act: Confronting the Legacies of Vaudeville and Minstrelsy." *Jazz Perspectives* 4, no. 3 (2010): 337–68.

Griswold, Robert. *Fatherhood in America: A History*. New York: Basic Books, 1993.

Hamilton, Andrew. "Adorno and the Autonomy of Art." In *Nostalgia for a Redeemed Future: Critical Theory*, edited by Stefano G. Ludovisi and Agostini G. Saavedra, 287–304. Rome: John Cabot University Press, 2009.

Hamilton, Carol. "All That Jazz Again: Adorno's Sociology of Music." *Popular Music and Society* 15, no. 3 (1991): 31–40.

Hammer, Epsen. *Adorno and the Political*. London: Routledge, 2006.

Harding, James Martin. "Adorno, Ellison, and the Critique of Jazz." *Cultural Critique* 31 (1995): 129–58.

Harker, Brian. *Louis Armstrong's Hot Five and Hot Seven Recordings*. New York: Oxford University Press, 2011.

Harney, Stefano, and Fred Moten. "Michael Brown." *boundary 2* 42, no. 4 (2015): 81–87.

———. *The Undercommons: Fugitive Planning and Black Study*. New York: Minor Compositions, 2013.

Harris, William. "'How You Sound?' Amiri Baraka Writes Free Jazz." In *Uptown Conversation: The New Jazz Studies*, edited by O'Meally, Edwards, and Griffin, 312–25. New York: Columbia University Press, 2004.

Hartman, Saidiya V. "The Position of the Unthought." Interview by Frank B. Wilderson III. *Qui Parle* 13, no. 2 (2003): 183–201.

———. *Scenes of Subjection: Terror, Slavery, and Self-Making in Nineteenth-Century America*. New York: Oxford University Press, 1997.

Hegel, Georg Wilhelm Friedrich. *Phenomenology of Spirit*. Oxford: Oxford University Press, 1977.

Heller, Michael. *Loft Jazz*. Oakland: University of California Press, 2016.

Henderson, Stephen. *Understanding the New Black Poetry: Black Speech and Black Music as Poetic References*. New York: Morrow, 1973.

Hentoff, Nat. "When I Pick Up That Horn, That's All: The Life and Music of Louis Armstrong." *Gadfly*, March/April 2000. www.gadflyonline.com/archive/marchapril00/archive-louisarmstrong.html.

Hersch, Charles. "Poisoning Their Coffee: Louis Armstrong and Civil Rights." *Polity* 34, no. 3 (2002): 371–92.

———. *Subversive Sounds: Race and the Birth of Jazz in New Orleans*. Chicago: University of Chicago Press, 2008.

Hewlett, Sylvia, and Cornel West. *The War Against Parents: What We Can Do for America's Beleaguered Moms and Dads*. Boston: Mariner, 1998.

Horkheimer, Max, and Theodor W. Adorno. *Dialectic of Enlightenment*. London: Verso, 1997.

Houck, Davis W., and Matthew A. Grindy. *Emmett Till and the Mississippi Press*. Jackson: University Press of Mississippi, 2007.

Iyer, Vijay. "Exploding the Narrative in Jazz Improvisation." In *Uptown Conversation: The New Jazz Studies*, edited by O'Meally, Edwards, and Griffin, 393–403. New York: Columbia University Press, 2004.

Jameson, Fredric. *Late Marxism: Adorno, or the Persistence of the Dialectic*. London: Verso, 2007.

———. "Reification and Utopia in Mass Culture." *Social Text* 1 (Winter 1979): 130–48.

Jenemann, David. *Adorno in America*. Minneapolis: University of Minnesota Press, 2007.

Jones, Meta DuEwa. *The Muse Is Music: Jazz Poetry from the Harlem Renaissance to Spoken Word*. Champaign: University of Illinois Press, 2011.

Jost, Ekkehard. *Free Jazz*. Graz: Perseus, 1974.

Kania, Andrew. "All Play and No Work: An Ontology of Jazz." *Journal of Aesthetics and Art Criticism* 69, no. 4 (2011): 391–403.

Kaufman, Bob. "Battle Report." In *Solitudes Crowded with Loneliness*, 8. New York: New Directions, 1965.

———. *Cranial Guitar: Selected Poems*. Minneapolis: Coffee House, 1996.

———. "O-Jazz-O War Memoir: Jazz, *Don't* Listen to It at Your Own Risk." In *Cranial Guitar*, 94–99.

Kelley, Robin D. G. "Introduction: A Poetics of Anticolonialism." In Aimé Césaire, *Discourse on Colonialism*, 7–28. New York: Monthly Review Press, 2000.

Kenney, William Howland. *Recorded Music in American Life: The Phonograph and Popular Memory, 1890–1945*. Oxford: Oxford University Press, 1999.

King, Martin Luther, Jr. "Dr. Martin Luther King Jr.'s Address to the 1964 Berlin Jazz Festival." *JazzTimes*, Jan. 21, 2008. https://jazztimes.com/news/dr-martin-luther-king-jr-s-address-to-the-1964-berlin-jazz-festival/.

Koenig, Karl, ed. *Jazz in Print (1859–1929): An Anthology of Selected Early Readings in Jazz History*. Hillsdale, NY: Pendragon, 2002.

Kofsky, Frank. *Black Music, White Business: Illuminating the History and Political Economy of Jazz*. New York: Pathfinder, 1988.

———. *John Coltrane and the Jazz Revolution of the 1960s*. New York: Pathfinder, 1998.

Kohli, Amor. "Saxophones and Smothered Rage: Bob Kaufman, Jazz and the Quest for Redemption." *Callaloo* 25, no. 1 (2002): 165–82.

Kouwenhoven, John. *Made in America: The Arts in Modern Civilization*. Garden City, NY: Doubleday, 1948.

———. "What's 'American' About America." In *The Jazz Cadence of American Culture*, edited by Robert G. O'Meally, 123–36. New York: Columbia University Press, 1998.

Levin, Thomas Y. "For the Record: Adorno on Music in the Age of Its Technological Reproducibility." *October* 55 (1990): 23–47.

Levinson, Daniel, Else Frenkel-Brunswik, Nevitt Sanford, and Theodor W. Adorno. *The Authoritarian Personality*. New York: Harper, 1950.

Lewandowski, Joseph. "Adorno on Jazz and Society." *Philosophy and Social Criticism* 22, no. 5 (1996): 103–21.

Lewis, George. "Improvised Music After 1950: Afrological and Eurological Perspectives." *Black Music Research Journal* 16, no. 1 (1996): 91–122.

———. *A Power Stronger Than Itself: The AACM and American Experimental Music*. Chicago: University of Chicago Press, 2008.

Liberman, Anatoly. "The Growth of the English Etymological Dictionary." In *Adventuring in Dictionaries: New Studies in the History of Lexicography*, edited by John Considine, 164–86. Newcastle: Cambridge Scholars, 2010.

———. "Our Habitat: Dwelling." *OUPblog*, Jan. 14, 2015. https://blog.oup.com/2015/01/dwelling-word-origin-etymology.

Lipsitz, George. "Songs of the Unsung: The Darby Hicks History of Jazz." In *Uptown Conversation: The New Jazz Studies*, edited by O'Meally, Edwards, and Griffin, 9–26. New York: Columbia University Press, 2004.

Mackey, Nathaniel. "Andoumboulouous Brush." In *Splay Anthem*, 3–7.

———. *Blue Fasa*. New York: New Directions, 2015.

———. "Cante moro." In *Paracritical Hinge: Talks, Notes, Interviews*, 188–198. Madison: University of Wisconsin Press, 2005.

———. *Discrepant Engagement: Dissonance, Cross-Culturality and Experimental Writing*. Cambridge: Cambridge University Press, 1993.

———. *Djbot Baghostus's Run*. Los Angeles: Sun and Moon, 1993.

———. "Epic World." Interview by Joseph Donahue. Poetry Foundation website. May 6, 2014. www.poetryfoundation.org/articles/70116/epic-world.

———. *From a Broken Bottle Traces of Perfume Still Emanate: Volumes 1–3*. New York: New Directions, 2010.

———. *Nod House*. New York: New Directions, 2011.

———. *Paracritical Hinge: Essays, Talks, Notes, Interviews*. Madison: University of Wisconsin Press, 2005.

———. "Song of the Andoumboulou: 24." In *Whatsaid Serif*, 40–43.

———. *Splay Anthem*. New York: New Directions, 2006.

———. *Whatsaid Serif*. San Francisco: City Lights, 1998.

Maclean, Robert. "After Modern Jazz: The Avant-Garde and Jazz Historiography." PhD diss., University of Michigan, 2011.

Madhubuti, Haki. *Don't Cry, Scream*. Detroit: Broadside, 1969.

Magee, Michael. *Emancipating Pragmatism: Emerson, Jazz, and Experimental Writing*. Tuscaloosa: University of Alabama Press, 2004.

"Marissa Janae Johnson Speaks: #BLM, Sanders & White Progressives™ | #TWIBnation." *This Week in Blackness*, August 10, 2015. www.youtube.com/watch?v=fQqdNF-BHTw.

Márkus, György. "Adorno and Mass Culture: Autonomous Art Against the Culture Industry." *Thesis Eleven* 86, no. 1 (2006): 67–89.

Marriott, David. *Haunted Life: Visual Culture and Black Modernity*. New Brunswick, NJ: Rutgers University Press, 2007.

Matlin, Daniel. "'Lift Up Yr Self!' Reinterpreting Amiri Baraka (LeRoi Jones), Black Power, and the Uplift Tradition." *Journal of American History* 93, no. 1 (2006): 91–116.

McClary, Susan. *Conventional Wisdom: The Content of Musical Form*. Berkeley: University of California Press, 2000.

McMichael, Robert. "'We Insist—Freedom Now!' Black Moral Authority, Jazz, and the Changeable Shape of Whiteness." *American Music* 16, no. 4 (1988): 375–416.

Mingus, Charles. *Beneath the Underdog*. Edinburgh: Canongate, 2011.

Misak, Cheryl. *The Oxford Handbook of American Philosophy*. Oxford: Oxford University Press, 2008.

Monson, Ingrid. "Doubleness and Jazz Improvisation: Irony, Parody, and Ethnomusicology." *Critical Inquiry* 20, no. 2 (1994): 283–313.

———. *Freedom Sounds: Civil Rights Call Out to Jazz and Africa*. Oxford: Oxford University Press, 2007.

———. "Riffs, Repetition, and Theories of Globalization." *Ethnomusicology* 43, no. 1 (1999): 31–65.

———. *Saying Something: Jazz Improvisation and Interaction*. Chicago: University of Chicago Press, 1996.

Moten, Fred. *B Jenkins*. Durham, NC: Duke University Press, 2010.

———. "Blackness and Nothingness (Mysticism in the Flesh)." *South Atlantic Quarterly* 112, no. 4 (2013): 737–80.

———. "Blackness and Poetry." *Evening Will Come*, no. 55 (July 2015): www.thevolta.org/ewc55-fmoten-p1.html.

———. "The Case of Blackness." *Criticism* 50, no. 2 (2008): 177–218.

———. "Fred Moten on Chris Ofili: Bluets, Black + Blue, In Lovely Blue." Lecture-performance presented at the New Museum (NY), Jan. 29, 2015. YouTube video. Posted by "New Museum," Nov. 30, 2015. www.youtube.com/watch?v=04aEVHhIVTw.

———. *In the Break: The Aesthetics of the Black Radical Tradition*. Minneapolis: University of Minnesota Press, 2003.

———. "The New International of Rhythmic Feeling(s)." *Thamyris/Intersecting: Place, Sex and Race* 18, no. 1 (2008): 31–56.

———. "The Subprime and the Beautiful." *African Identities* 11, no. 2 (2013): 237–45.

———. "To Consent Not to Be a Single Being." Poetry Foundation website. Feb. 15, 2010. www.poetryfoundation.org/harriet/2010/02/to-consent-not-to-be-a-single-being.

Moten, Fred, and Charles Henry Rowell. "'Words Don't Go There': An Interview with Fred Moten." *Callaloo* 27, no. 4 (2004): 954–66.

Nesbitt, Nick. "Sounding Autonomy: Adorno, Coltrane and Jazz." *Telos* 116 (Summer 1999): 81–98.

Nielsen, Aldon Lynn. *Black Chant: Languages of African-American Postmodernism*. Cambridge: Cambridge University Press, 1997.

Oakland, Daniel. "Remembering in Jazz: Collective Memory and Collective Improvisation." *Lambda Alpha Journal* 28 (1998): 16–27.

Okiji, Fumi. "Storytelling in Jazz Work as Retrospective Collaboration." *Journal of the Society for American Music* 11, no. 1 (2017): 70–92.

O'Meally, Robert G., Brent Hayes Edwards, and Farah Jasmine Griffin, eds. *Uptown Conversation: The New Jazz Studies*. New York: Columbia University Press, 2004.

Ostendorf, Berndt. "Minstrelsy & Early Jazz." *Massachusetts Review* 20, no. 3 (1979): 574–602.

Paddison, Max. *Adorno's Aesthetics of Music*. Cambridge: Cambridge University Press, 1993.

———. "The Critique Criticised: Adorno and Popular Music." *Popular Music* 2 (1982): 201–18.

———. "Mimesis and the Aesthetics of Musical Expression." *Music Analysis* 29, nos. 1–3 (2010): 126–48.

Panassié, Hugues. *Hot Jazz*. London: Cassell, 1936.

Patke, Rajeev. "Benjamin on Art and Reproducibility: The Case of Music." In *Walter Benjamin and Art*, edited by Andrew Benjamin, 185–208. London: Continuum, 2005.

Patterson, Orlando. *Slavery and Social Death: A Comparative Study*. Cambridge, MA: Harvard University Press, 1990.

Paudyal, Bed. "Mimesis in Adorno's Aesthetic Theory." *Journal of Philosophy* 4, no. 8 (2009): 1–10.

Pavlić, Edward. *Crossroads Modernism: Descent and Emergence in African-American Literary Culture*. Minneapolis: University of Minnesota Press, 2002.

Perchard, Tom. "Hugues Panassié Contra Walter Benjamin: Bodies, Masses and the Iconic Jazz Recording in Mid-Century France." *Popular Music and Society* 35, no. 3 (2012): 375–98.

———. "Tradition, Modernity and the Supernatural Swing: Re-reading Primitivism in Hugues Panassié's Writing on Jazz." *Popular Music* 30, no. 1 (2011): 25–45.

Peretti, Burton. *The Creation of Jazz: Music, Race, and Culture in Urban America*. Champaign: University of Illinois Press, 1992.

Peters, Gary. *The Philosophy of Improvisation*. Chicago: University of Chicago Press, 2009.

Philip, M. NourbeSe, *Zong!* Middletown, CT: Wesleyan University Press, 2008.

Porter, Eric. *What Is This Thing Called Jazz? African American Musicians as Artists, Critics, and Activists*. Berkeley: University of California Press, 2002.

Porter, Lewis. "John Coltrane's *A Love Supreme*: Jazz Improvisation as Composition." *Journal of the American Musicological Society* 38, no. 3 (1985): 593–621.

Priestley, Brian. *Jazz on Record: A History*. New York: Billboard, 1991.

———. *Mingus: A Critical Biography*. New York: Da Capo, 1983.

Radano, Ronald M. *Lying up a Nation: Race and Black Music*. Chicago: University of Chicago Press, 2003.

———. *New Musical Figurations: Anthony Braxton's Cultural Critique*. Chicago: University of Chicago Press, 1993.

Robinson, J. Bradford. "The Jazz Essays of Theodor Adorno: Some Thoughts on Jazz Reception in Weimar Germany." *Popular Music* 13, no. 1 (1994): 1–25.

Sargeant, Winthrop. *Jazz, Hot and Hybrid*. New York: Da Capo, 1975.

Saul, Scott. *Freedom Is, Freedom Ain't: Jazz and the Making of the Sixties*. Cambridge, MA: Harvard University Press, 2003.

Sawyer, Keith. "Improvisational Cultures: Collaborative Emergence and Creativity in Improvisation." *Mind, Culture, and Activity* 7, no. 3 (2000): 180–85.

Schonherr, Ulrich. "Adorno and Jazz: Reflections on a Failed Encounter." *Telos* 87 (March 1991): 85–96.

Schuller, Gunther. *Musings: The Musical Worlds of G. Schuller*. New York: Oxford University Press, 1989.

———. "Sonny Rollins and the Challenge of Thematic Improvisation." *Jazz Review* 1, no. 1 (1958): 6–11.

———. *The Swing Era: The Development of Jazz, 1930–1945*. New York: Oxford University Press, 1991.

Sexton, Jared. "Ante-Anti-Blackness: Afterthoughts." *Lateral* 1 (2012): https://circuitdebater.wikispaces.com/file/view/ante-anti-blackness-+afterthoughts.pdf.

———. "People-of-Color-Blindness: A Lecture by Jared Sexton." University of California, Berkeley, n.d. YouTube video. Posted by UC Berkeley Events, Oct. 27, 2011. www.youtube.com/watch?v=qNVMI3oiDaI.

———. "The Social Life of Social Death: On Afro-pessimism and Black Optimism." *In-Tensions* 5 (2011): www.yorku.ca/intent/issue5/articles/jaredsexton.php.

Shepp, Archie. "An Artist Speaks Bluntly." *Downbeat*, Dec. 16, 1965, 11.

Shim, Eunmi. *Lennie Tristano: His Life in Music*. Ann Arbor: University of Michigan Press, 2007.

Sidran, Ben. *Black Talk*. New York: Da Capo, 1981.

Siebert, Rudolf. *Manifesto of the Critical Theory of Society and Religion*. Vol. 2. Leiden: Brill, 2010.

Sinnreich, Aram. "All That Jazz Was: Remembering the Mainstream Avant-Garde." *American Quarterly* 57, no. 2 (2005): 561–72.

Snead, James. "On Repetition in Black Culture." *Black American Literature Forum* 15, no. 4 (1981): 146–54.

Solis, Gabriel. "Hearing Monk: History, Memory, and the Making of a 'Jazz Giant.'" *Musical Quarterly* 86, no. 1 (2002): 82–116.

———. "'A Unique Chunk of Jazz Reality': Authorship, Musical Work Concepts, and Thelonious Monk's Live Recordings from the Five Spot, 1958." *Ethnomusicology* 43, no. 3 (2004): 315–47.

Spillers, Hortense J. "'All the Things You Could Be by Now, If Sigmund Freud's Wife Was Your Mother': Psychoanalysis and Race." In *Black, White, and in Color*, 376–427.

———. *Black, White, and in Color: Essays on American Literature and Culture*. Chicago: University Of Chicago Press, 2003.

———. "The Crisis of the Negro Intellectual: A Post-Date." In *Black, White, and in Color*, 152–75.

———. "The Idea of Black Culture." *CR: The New Centennial Review* 6, no. 3 (2006): 7–28.

———. "'Mama's Baby, Papa's Maybe: American Grammar Book." In *Black, White, and in Color*, 203–29.

———. "Moving On Down the Line: Variations on the African-American Sermon." In *Black, White, and in Color*, 251–76.

Stearns, Marshall. "Ours to Offer." *Altoona (PA) Tribune*, August 10, 1956. www.newspapers.com/newspage/57846467/.

Stein, David. "Negotiating Primitivist Modernisms: Louis Armstrong, Robert Goffin, and the Transatlantic Jazz Debate." *European Journal of American Studies* 6, no. 2 (2011): 1–15.

———. "The Performance of Jazz Autobiography." *Genre* 37, no. 2 (2004): 173–99.

Steinbeck, Paul. "Intermusicality, Humor, and Cultural Critique in the Art Ensemble of Chicago's *A Jackson in Your House*." *Jazz Perspectives* 5, no. 2 (2011): 135–54.

Steinman, Clay. "Beyond Eurocentrism: The Frankfurt School and Whiteness Theory." In *Globalizing Critical Theory*, edited by Max Pensky, 115–37. Lanham, MD: Rowman and Littlefield, 2004.

Stepto, Robert Burns. *From Behind the Veil: A Study of Afro-American Narrative*. Urbana: University of Illinois Press, 1991.

Subotnik, Rose Rosengard. *Deconstructive Variations: Music and Reason in Western Society*. Minneapolis: University of Minnesota Press, 1996.

Switzer, Robert. "Signifying the Blues." *Alif: Journal of Comparative Poetics* 21 (2001): 25–76.

Taylor, Arthur. *Notes and Tone*. New York: Perigee, 1977.

Thomas, Lorenzo. *Don't Deny My Name: Words and Music and the Black Intellectual Tradition*. Ann Arbor: University of Michigan Press, 2008.

Walser, Robert. "Out of Notes: Signification, Interpretation, and the Problem of Miles Davis." In Gabbard, *Jazz Among the Discourses*, 165–88.

Washington, Salim. "'All the Things You Could Be by Now': *Charles Mingus Presents Charles Mingus* and the Limits of Avant-Garde Jazz." In *Uptown Conversation: The New Jazz Studies*, edited by O'Meally, Edwards, and Griffin, 27–49. New York: Columbia University Press, 2004.

Weheliye, Alexander. *Phonographies: Grooves in Sonic Afro-Modernity*. Durham, NC: Duke University Press, 2005.

Weinstein, Norman. "Steps Toward an Integrative Comprehension of the Art Ensemble of Chicago's Music." *Lenox Avenue: A Journal of Interarts Inquiry* 3 (1997): 5–11.

Wellmer, Albrecht. "Truth, Semblance, Reconciliation: Adorno's Aesthetic Redemption of Modernity." In *The Frankfurt School: Critical Assessments*, edited by Jay Bernstein, 4:29–54. London: Routledge, 1994.

Werner, Craig Hansen. *Playing the Changes: From Afro-Modernism to the Jazz Impulse*. Urbana: University of Illinois Press, 1994.

White, Shane, and Graham J. White. *The Sounds of Slavery: Discovering African American History Through Songs, Sermons, and Speech*. Boston: Beacon, 2005.

Wilcock, Evelyn. "Adorno, Jazz and Racism: 'Über Jazz' and the 1934–7 British Jazz Debate." *Telos* 107 (March 1996): 63–80.

Wilderson, Frank B., III. *Red, White and Black: Cinema and the Structure of U.S. Antagonisms*. Durham, NC: Duke University Press, 2010.

———. *Incognegro: A Memoir of Exile and Apartheid*. New York: South End, 2008.

Williams, Jessica. "Thelonious Sphere Monk." Jessica Williams—Currents, March 1998. www.jessicawilliams.com/currents/monk.html.

Williams, Martin. *The Jazz Tradition*. New York: Oxford University Press, 1993.

Witkin, Robert. *Adorno on Music*. London: Routledge, 1998.

———. *Adorno on Popular Culture*. London: Routledge, 2003.

———. "Why Did Adorno 'Hate' Jazz?" *Sociological Theory* 18, no. 1 (2000): 145–70.

Zamir, Shamoon. *Dark Voices: W. E. B. Du Bois and American Thought, 1888–1903*. Chicago: University of Chicago Press, 1995.

Zuidervaart, Lambert. *Adorno's Aesthetic Theory: Redemption of Illusion*. Cambridge, MA: MIT Press, 1993.

———. "The Social Significance of Autonomous Art: Adorno and Bürger." *Journal of Aesthetics and Art Criticism* 48, no. 1 (1990): 61–77.

DISCOGRAPHY

Armstrong, Louis. "Ain't Misbehavin'"/"(What Did I Do to Be So) Black and Blue." Composed by Thomas (Fats) Waller and Harry Brooks, lyrics by Andy Razaf. OKeh 8714, 1929, 78 rpm, Shellac 10″.

Armstrong, Louis. "(What Did I Do to Be So) Black and Blue." On *Louis Armstrong in Philadelphia 1949*. Composed by Thomas (Fats) Waller and Harry Brooks, lyrics by Andy Razaf. Jazz Anthology JA 5190, 1981 [1949], vinyl.

Armstrong, Louis, and His All-Stars. "(What Did I Do to Be So) Black and Blue." On *Satch Plays Fats: A Tribute to the Immortal Fats Waller*. Composed by Thomas (Fats) Waller and Harry Brooks, lyrics by Andy Razaf. Columbia/Legacy CK 64927, 2000 [1955], compact disc.

Armstrong, Louis. "(What Did I Do to Be So) Black and Blue"/"Blue Again." "Black and Blue" composed by Thomas (Fats) Waller and Harry Brooks, lyrics by Andy Razaf. "Blue Again" composed by Jimmy McHugh, lyrics by Dorothy Fields. Vocalion 3115, 1937, 78 rpm, Shellac 10″.

Armstrong, Louis, and His Orchestra. "(What Did I Do to Be So) Black and Blue"/"I Can't Give You Anything but Love." "Black and Blue" composed by Thomas (Fats) Waller and Harry Brooks, lyrics by Andy Razaf. "Anything but Love" composed by Jimmy McHugh, lyrics by Dorothy Fields. Columbia 38052, 1947, Shellac 10″.

Art Ensemble of Chicago. "Dexterity." On *Message to Our Folks*. Composed by Charlie Parker. Sunspots SPOT 549, 2004 [1969], compact disc.

Art Ensemble of Chicago. *Message to Our Folks*. Lester Bowie (trumpet, percussion), Malachi Favors Maghostut (bass, percussion, vocals), Joseph Jarman (saxophones, clarinets, percussion), Roscoe Mitchell (saxophones, clarinets, flute, percussion). Sunspots SPOT 549, 2004 [1969], compact disc.

Art Ensemble of Chicago. "Old Time Religion." On *Message to Our Folks*. Composed by Roscoe Mitchell. Sunspots SPOT 549, 2004 [1969], compact disc.

Ayler, Albert. *Ghosts*. Albert Ayler (tenor saxophone), Don Cherry (cornet), Gary Peacock (bass), Sonny Murray (drums). Fontana SFJL 925, 1969 [1965], LP.

Ayler, Albert. "Mothers." On *Ghosts*. Composed by Albert Ayler. Fontana SFJL 925, 1969 [1965], LP.

Bartók, Béla. *Music for String Instruments, Percussion and Celesta*. Bavarian Radio Symphony Orchestra. Conducted by Rafael Kubelik. Orfeo #551011, 2011, compact disc.

Berry, Chu, and His Little Jazz Ensemble. "Body and Soul." On *Chu Berry, 1937–1941*. Artie Shapiro (bass), Sidney Catlett (drums), Danny Barker (guitar), Clyde Hart (piano), Roy Eldridge (trumpet). Composed by Johnny Green. Classics 784, 1994, compact disc.

Berry, Chu, and His Little Jazz Ensemble. *Chu Berry, 1937–1941*. Classics 784, 1994, compact disc.

Brown, Clifford. *With Strings*. Clifford Brown (trumpet), Richie Powell (piano), Max Roach (drums), George Morrow (double bass), Barry Galbraith (guitar), Neal Hefti (arranger, conductor). Verve 558 078-2, 1998 [1955], compact disc.

Carter, Betty. *Betty Carter at the Village Vanguard*. Betty Carter (vocals), Norman Simmons (piano), Lisle Atkinson (bass), Al Harewood (drums). Bet-Car/MK 1001, 1970, LP.

Carter, Betty. "Body and Soul." On *Betty Carter at the Village Vanguard*. Composed by Johnny Green, lyrics by Edward Heyman, Robert Sour, and Frank Eyton. Bet-Car/MK 1001, 1970, LP.

Carter, Betty. "Heart and Soul." On *Betty Carter at the Village Vanguard*. Composed by Hoagy Carmichael, lyrics by Frank Loesser. Bet-Car/MK 1001, 1970, LP.

Chopin, Frédéric. "Marche funèbre." On *Préludes / Piano Sonata No. 2*. Martha Argerich (piano). Deutsche Grammophon 00289 477 8380, 2009, compact disc.

Coleman, Ornette. "Beauty Is a Rare Thing." On *This Is Our Music*. Composed by Ornette Coleman. Atlantic 1353, 2005 [1961], compact disc.

Coleman, Ornette. *Free Jazz: A Collective Improvisation*. Ornette Coleman (alto saxophone), Don Cherry (pocket trumpet), Scott LaFaro (bass), Billy Higgins (drums), Eric Dolphy (bass clarinet), Freddie Hubbard (trumpet), Charlie Haden (bass), Ed Blackwell (drums). Atlantic Jazz 7567-81347-2 YG, 2004 [1961], compact disc.

Coleman, Ornette. *The Shape of Jazz to Come*. Ornette Coleman (alto saxophone), Don Cherry (cornet), Charlie Haden (bass), Billy Higgins (drums). Essential Jazz Classics EJC55450, 2010 [1959], compact disc.

Coleman, Ornette. *This Is Our Music*. Ornette Coleman (alto saxophone), Don Cherry (trumpet), Charlie Haden (double bass), Ed Blackwell (drums). Atlantic 1353, 2005 [1961], compact disc.

Coltrane, John. *Ascension*. John Coltrane (tenor saxophone), McCoy Tyner (piano), Jimmy Garrison (bass), Elvin Jones (drums), Freddie Hubbard (trumpet), Dewey Johnson (trumpet), Marion Brown (alto saxophone), John Tchicai (alto saxophone), Pharoah Sanders (tenor saxophone), Archie Shepp (tenor saxophone), Art Davis (bass). Impulse! AS-95, 2009 [1965], compact disc.

Coltrane, John. "Body and Soul." *Coltrane's Sound.* Composed by Johnny Green. Atlantic 8122-73754-2, 2000 [1964], compact disc.

Coltrane, John. *Coltrane's Sound.* John Coltrane (tenor saxophone, soprano saxophone), McCoy Tyner (piano), Steve Davis (bass), Elvin Jones (drums). Atlantic 8122-73754-2, 2000 [1964], compact disc.

Coltrane, John. "Giant Steps (alternative version), Take 1 [incomplete]." On *Heavyweight Champion: The Complete Atlantic Recordings.* John Coltrane (tenor saxophone), Tommy Flanagan (piano), Paul Chambers (bass), Art Taylor (drums). Composed by John Coltrane. Rhino Homemade, RHM1 7784, 2000, compact disc.

Coltrane, John. *Heavyweight Champion: The Complete Atlantic Recordings.* Rhino Homemade, RHM1 7784, 2000, compact disc.

Coltrane, John. *A Love Supreme.* John Coltrane (tenor saxophone), Jimmy Garrison (double bass), Elvin Jones (drums, gong, timpani), McCoy Tyner (piano); alternate takes of "Acknowledgement": Art Davis (double bass), Archie Shepp (tenor saxophone). Impulse! 589 945-2, 2002 [1965], compact disc.

Coltrane, John. *Meditations.* John Coltrane (tenor saxophone), Pharoah Sanders (tenor saxophone), McCoy Tyner (piano), Jimmy Garrison (double bass), Elvin Jones (drums), Rashied Ali (drums). Impulse! 0602517920378, 2009 [1966], compact disc.

Coltrane, John. *Sun Ship.* John Coltrane (tenor saxophone, soprano saxophone), McCoy Tyner (piano), Jimmy Garrison (bass), Elvin Jones (drums). Impulse! B0018075-02, 2013 [1971], compact disc.

Coltrane, John. "Sun Ship." On *Sun Ship.* Impulse! B0018075-02, 2013 [1971], compact disc.

Davis, Miles. "It Never Entered My Mind." On *Workin' with the Miles Davis Quintet.* Composed by Richard Rodgers. Prestige TCJ2 53062, 2006 [1959], compact disc.

Davis, Miles. *Workin' with the Miles Davis Quintet.* Miles Davis (trumpet), John Coltrane (tenor saxophone), Red Garland (piano), Paul Chambers (bass, cello), Philly Joe Jones (drums). Prestige TCJ2 53062, 2006 [1956], compact disc.

Ellington, Duke. "Fleurette Africaine (African Flower)." On *Money Jungle.* Composed by Duke Ellington. Blue Note 7243 5 38227 2 9, 2002 [1963], compact disc.

Ellington, Duke. *Money Jungle.* Duke Ellington (piano), Charles Mingus (double bass), Max Roach (drums). Blue Note 7243 5 38227 2 9, 2002 [1963], compact disc.

Ellington, Duke, and His Washingtonians. "East St Louis Toodle-O / Hop Head." "Toodle-O" composed by Duke Ellington and Bubber Miley. "Hop Head" composed by Duke Ellington and Otto Hardwicke. Parlophone R 2202, Shellac 10″.

Gordon, Dexter. "Body and Soul." On *Nights at the Keystone, Volume 3.* Dexter Gordon (tenor saxophone), George Cables (piano), Rufus Reid (bass), Eddie Gladden (drums). Composed by Johnny Green. Blue Note CDP 7 94850 2, 1990 [1978], compact disc.

Hawkins, Coleman. *Body and Soul.* Coleman Hawkins (tenor saxophone), Tommy Lindsay (trumpet), Joe Guy (trumpet), Early Hardy (trombone), Jackie Fields (alto saxophone), Eustis Moore (alto saxophone), Gene Rodgers (piano), William Oscar

Smith (double bass), Arthur Herbert (drums), Thelma Carpenter (vocals). Victor Records/RCA 09026685152, 1996, compact disc.

Hawkins, Coleman. "Body and Soul." On *Body and Soul.* Composed by Johnny Green. Victor Records/RCA 09026685152, 1996, compact disc.

Holiday, Billie. "Body and Soul." On *Body and Soul.* Composed by Johnny Green, lyrics by Edward Heyman, Robert Sour, and Frank Eyton. Verve 314 589 308-2, 2002 [1957], compact disc.

Holiday, Billie. *Body and Soul.* Billie Holiday (vocals), Ben Webster (tenor saxophone), Barney Kessel (guitar), Harry "Sweets" Edison (trumpet), Jimmy Rowles (piano), Red Mitchell (bass), Larry Bunker (drums). Verve 314 589 308-2, 2002 [1957], compact disc.

Holiday, Billie. *The Complete Decca Recordings.* MCA Records GRP 26012, 1991, 2 compact discs.

Holiday, Billie. "I Loves You, Porgy." 1948. On *The Complete Decca Recordings.* Billie Holiday (vocals), Bobby Tucker (piano), John Levy (bass), Denzil Best (drums), and Mindell Lowe (guitar). Composed by George Gershwin, lyrics by Ira Gershwin. MCA Records GRP 26012, 1991, compact disc 2, track 6.

Holiday, Billie, featuring the Gordon Jenkins Orchestra. "You're My Thrill." On *The Complete Decca Recordings.* Composed by Jay Gorney, lyrics by Sidney Clare. MCA Records GRP 26012, 1991, compact disc.

Holiday, Billie, with Ray Ellis and his orchestra. "I'm a Fool to Want You." On *Lady in Satin.* Composed by Jack Wolf, Joel Herron, and Frank Sinatra. Columbia/Legacy 88697 492002, 2009 [1958], compact disc.

Holiday, Billie, with Ray Ellis and his orchestra. *Lady in Satin.* Columbia/Legacy 88697 492002, 2009 [1958], compact disc.

House, Eddie "Son." "Dry Spell Blues Part I / Dry Spell Blues Part II." Paramount 12990, 1930, Shellac 10″.

Jefferson, Eddie. *Body and Soul.* Eddie Jefferson (vocals), Dave Burns (trumpet), James Moody (tenor saxophone, flute), Barry Harris (piano), Steve Davis (bass), Bill English (drums). Prestige UCCO-9477, 2008, compact disc.

Jefferson, Eddie. "Body and Soul." On *Body and Soul.* Composed by Johnny Green, lyrics by Edward Heyman, Robert Sour, and Frank Eyton. Prestige UCCO-9477, 2008, compact disc.

Marsalis, Wynton. *Citi Movement (Griot New York).* Wynton Marsalis (trumpet), Wycliffe Gordon (trombone), Wessell Anderson (alto), Todd Williams (soprano and tenor), Eric Reed (piano), Reginald Veal (double bass), Herlin Riley (drums), Herbert Harris (tenor saxophone), Marthaniel Roberts (piano). Columbia, COL 473055 2, 1993, compact disc.

Marsalis, Wynton. "The Legend of Buddy Bolden." On *Citi Movement (Griot New York).* Composed by Wynton Marsalis. Columbia, COL 473055 2, 1993, compact disc.

Mingus, Charles. *Charles Mingus Presents Charles Mingus.* Charles Mingus (double bass), Ted Curson (trumpet), Eric Dolphy (alto saxophone and bass clarinet), Dannie Richmond (drums). Candid CCD 79005, 2000 [1960], compact disc.

Mingus, Charles. *The Clown*. Charles Mingus (bass), Shafi Hadi (alto and tenor saxophones), Jimmy Knepper (trombone), Wade Legge (piano), Dannie Richmond (drums), Jean Shepherd (narration). Rhino Records 8122-79641-5, 2013 [1957], compact disc.

Mingus, Charles. "The Clown." On *The Clown*. Composed by Charles Mingus. Rhino Records 8122-79641-5, 2013 [1957], compact disc.

Mingus, Charles. "Fables of Faubus." On *Charles Mingus Presents Charles Mingus*. Composed by Charles Mingus. Candid CCD 79005, 2000 [1960], compact disc.

Mingus, Charles. "Fables of Faubus." On *Mingus Ah Um*. Composed by Charles Mingus. Columbia 88697127572, 2007 [1959], compact disc.

Mingus, Charles. "Haitian Fight Song." On *The Clown*. Composed by Charles Mingus. Rhino Records 8122-79641-5, 2013 [1957], compact disc.

Mingus, Charles. *Mingus Ah Um*. John Handy (alto saxophone: 6, 7, 9, 10, 11, 12; clarinet: 8; tenor sax: 1, 2), Booker Ervin (tenor saxophone), Shafi Hadi (tenor saxophone: 2, 3, 4, 7, 8, 10; alto saxophone: 1, 5, 6, 9, 12), Willie Dennis (trombone: 3, 4, 5, 12), Jimmy Knepper (trombone: 1, 7, 8, 9, 10), Horace Parlan (piano), Charles Mingus (bass, piano), Dannie Richmond (drums). Columbia 88697127572, 2007 [1959], compact disc.

Mingus, Charles, with Eric Dolphy. *Cornell 1964*. Eric Dolphy (bass clarinet, alto saxophone, flute), Ted Curson (trumpet), Clifford Jordon (tenor saxophone), Jaki Byard (piano), Charles Mingus (double bass), Dannie Richmond (drums). Blue Note 0946 3 92210 2 8, 2007 [1964], compact disc.

Mingus, Charles, with Eric Dolphy. "Fables of Faubus." On *Cornell 1964*. Composed by Charles Mingus. Blue Note 0946 3 92210 2 8, 2007 [1964], compact disc.

Mingus, Charles, with Eric Dolphy. "Meditations." On *Cornell 1964*. Composed by Charles Mingus. Blue Note 0946 3 92210 2 8, 2007 [1964], compact disc.

Mingus, Charles, with Eric Dolphy. "Orange Was the Color of Her Dress, Then Blue Silk." On *Cornell 1964*. Composed by Charles Mingus. Blue Note 0946 3 92210 2 8, 2007 [1964], compact disc.

Mingus, Charles, with Eric Dolphy. "Sophisticated Lady." On *Cornell 1964*. Blue Note 0946 3 92210 2 8, 2007 [1964], compact disc.

Mingus, Charles, with Eric Dolphy. "What Love." On *Charles Mingus Presents Charles Mingus*. Composed by Charles Mingus. Candid CCD 79005, 2000 [1960], compact disc.

Monk, Thelonious. *Genius of Modern Music*, Vol. 1. Thelonious Monk (piano), Art Blakey (drums), Idrees Sulieman (trumpet: 1–6), Danny Quebec West (alto saxophone: 1–6), Billy Smith (tenor saxophone: 1–6), Gene Ramey (bass: 1–16), George Taitt (trumpet: 17–21), Sahib Shihab (alto saxophone: 17–21), Bob Paige (bass: 17–21). Blue Note 7243 5 32138 2 4, 2001 [1947], compact disc.

Monk, Thelonious. "Monk's Mood." On *Genius of Modern Music*, Vol. 2. Composed by Thelonious Monk. Blue Note 4971832, 1998 [1956], compact disc.

Monk, Thelonious. "Round Midnight." On *Genius of Modern Music*, Vol. 1. Composed by Thelonious Monk. Blue Note 7243 5 32138 2 4, 2001 [1947], compact disc.

Original Dixieland Jass Band. "Dixieland Jass Band One Step / Livery Stable Blues." Victor 18255, 1917, Shellac 10″.

Parker, Charlie. *Charlie Parker with Strings*. Verve/Universal MG C-675, 2013, compact disc.

Roach, Max. "Triptych." On *We Insist! Max Roach's Freedom Now Suite*. Candid CCD 79002, 1990 [1960], compact disc.

Roach, Max. *We Insist! Max Roach's Freedom Now Suite*. Max Roach (drums), Abbey Lincoln (vocals), Booker Little (trumpet), Julian Priester (trombone), Walter Benton (tenor saxophone), Coleman Hawkins (tenor saxophone), James Schenk (bass), Michael Olatunji (congas, vocals), Raymond Mantilla (percussion), Tomas du Vall (percussion). Candid CCD 79002, 1990 [1960], compact disc.

Rollins, Sonny. "Blue 7." On *Saxophone Colossus*. Composed by Sonny Rollins. Prestige 0025218810524, 2006 [1958], compact disc.

Rollins, Sonny. *Freedom Suite*. Sonny Rollins (tenor saxophone), Oscar Pettiford (bass), Max Roach (drums). Riverside Records 0888072305076, [1958] 2008, compact disc.

Rollins, Sonny. *Saxophone Colossus*. Sonny Rollins (tenor saxophone), Tommy Flanagan (piano), Doug Watkins (bass), Max Roach (drums). Prestige 0025218810524, 2006 [1958], compact disc.

Schoenberg, Arnold. *Pierrot lunaire*. Ensemble InterContemporain, Christine Schäfer (soprano), David Pittman-Jennings (baritone). Conducted by Pierre Boulez. *Pierrot lunaire / Herzgewächse / Ode to Napoleon*. Deutsche Grammophon 0289 457 6302 6, 1998, compact disc.

Shepp, Archie. "Body and Soul." On *Yasmina: A Black Woman*. Composed by Johnny Green. Charly Records, Le Jazz CD 51, 1996 [1969], compact disc.

Shepp, Archie. *Fire Music*. Archie Shepp (tenor saxophone), Ted Curson (trumpet), Joseph Orange (trombone), Marion Brown (alto saxophone), Reggie Johnson (double bass), Joe Chambers (drums), David Izenzon (double bass on track 3), J.C. Moses (drums on track 3). Impulse! IMP 11582, 1995 [1965], compact disc.

Shepp, Archie. *The Magic of Ju-Ju*. Archie Shepp (tenor saxophone), Martin Banks (trumpet, flugelhorn), Mike Zwerin (bass trombone, trombone), Reggie Workman (bass), Norman Connors (drums), Beaver Harris (drums), Frank Charles (talking drum), Dennis Charles (percussion), Ed Blackwell (rhythm logs). Impulse! UCCU-9297, 2006 [1968], compact disc.

Shepp, Archie. "The Magic of Ju-Ju." On *The Magic of Ju-Ju*. Composed by Archie Shepp. Impulse! UCCU-9297, 2006 [1968], compact disc.

Shepp, Archie. "Malcolm, Malcolm—Semper Malcolm." On *Fire Music*. Composed by Archie Shepp. Impulse! IMP 11582, 1995 [1965], compact disc.

Shepp, Archie. *Yasmina: A Black Woman*. Archie Shepp (tenor saxophone, vocals), Clifford Thornton (cornet), Lester Bowie (trumpet), Arthur Jones (alto saxophone), Roscoe Mitchell (bass saxophone, piccolo), Dave Burrell (piano), Malachi Favors (bass), Earl Freeman (bass), Sunny Murray (drums, percussion), Art Taylor (rhythm logs), Laurence Devereaux (balafon). Charly Records, Le Jazz CD 51, 1996 [1969], compact disc.

Smith, Bessie. "Gimme a Pigfoot" / "Take Me for a Buggy Ride." OKeh 8949, 1933, Shellac 10″.

Smith, Bessie. "Nobody Knows You When You're Down and Out." Parlophone R2481, 1933, Shellac 10″.

Waters, Ethel, and Clarence Williams. "West End Blues." Columbia 14365-D, 1928, 10″.

Whiteman, Paul, and His Orchestra / The Virginians. "Hot Lips (He's Got Hot Lips When He Plays Jazz)" / "Send Back My Honeymoon." Victor 18920, 1922, Shellac 10″.

Wilson, Cassandra. "Body and Soul." On *She Who Weeps*. Composed by Johnny Green, lyrics by Edward Heyman, Robert Sour, and Frank Eyton. JMT Productions 834 443-2, 1991, compact disc.

Wilson, Cassandra. *She Who Weeps*. Cassandra Wilson (vocals, drum programming), Jean-Paul Bourelly (guitar), Herman Fowlkes (bass), Kevin Bruce Harris (bass), Reggie Washington (bass), Rod Williams (piano), Mark Johnson (drums), Tani Tabbal (drums). JMT Productions 834 443-2, 1991, compact disc.

INDEX

Lightning Source UK Ltd.
Milton Keynes UK
UKHW010115290421
382820UK00001B/25

9 781503 605855